The Nature of Truth

Defining Truth, Knowledge & the Good

By

Christopher Angle

ISBN 979-8-9877707-6-4
Library of Congress Catalog No. 97-92853

Published by RITE Report Inc.
100 Research Dr., Unit 16
Stamford, CT 06906
tel. 203/253-2008
email: detmar.haskell@icloud.com

Other Detmar & Haskell Dialogues by Christopher Angle in chronological order

- *The Nature of Aesthetics*
- *The Nature of Ethics*
- *The Philosophical Equations of Economics*
- *The Nature of the Political Left & Right*

Table of Contents

Prologue

The principals of the following dialogue, Detmar and Haskell, first appeared in *The Nature of Aesthetics* followed by Dialogue#2 entitled, *The Nature of Ethics.* In each encounter Haskell brought with him a problem of philosophical import and a set of questions and solicits Detmar, a botany professor who has a penchant for philosophy, to provide solutions.

Subsequent to the inquiry into ethics, Haskell has another conundrum that arises out of the previous discussion that he needs to address, and finding it a difficult task for solution, he has again come to Detmar.

Chapter One

Experience and Information

Haskell arrives at the office door of Detmar which is open. Detmar looks up, and the following transpires.

Haskell: Professor!

Detmar: Haskell, how are you? Come on in.

H: Thank you very much.

D: Well, it's been a while. What's new? How are your studies?

H: Everything is going well. I have started my dissertation and am proceeding to matriculate through my graduate curriculum.

D: Good.

H: Yes, and I must thank you because you have been a great influence and your thoughts pervade the subject matters upon which I expound and scribe for my professors.

D: Well, I am glad to hear it and proud to be a part of it.

H: Since our last time together when we spoke of ethics and judgment, I have been trying to satisfy myself regarding one of the topics that we touched upon, but unfortunately, I have not been able to assimilate it fully to my satisfaction. It still lurks in me, and when I have become involved with my fellow students and peers, I have not been able to express myself adequately enough to satisfy their questions and comments about the subject.

D: And, what is that subject?

H: In our last discussion on ethics I made the inquiry about how we know our conclusions are for sure. I asked that when we come to our conclusions and find the standard that allows us to understand beauty or ethics, or the study of good and bad in behavior, how do we know that we are right? How do we know that we know more than the next guy about this subject or any other? How do we know when we have stumbled across knowledge or something that is true so that we may say to all that this is true or that we have definite knowledge pertaining to that?

D: Do you remember how I responded?

H: Yes. You said that we must consider the subject of inquiry completely, and over time with the examination of our ideas, their validity will surface and become more accepted and stronger overall, and we may become more confident that we are correct and right. And if we are not, eventually our ideas will be usurped and eclipsed by others which will lead further to whether something is true or not.

D: Yes.

H: You seemed to say that the probability of the trueness of our ideas becomes greater as the examination over time brings assurance that they become true.

D: Yes, that is correct.

H: This makes me wonder whether truth and knowledge are not somehow tied to probability. And so, I am wondering what is the nature of that which is true. What, I wonder, are truth and knowledge? Do you have a definition of them, or is there a standard we can put forth so that we may judge that which is true and of what we have knowledge and can know?

D: Surely. Knowledge is the assimilation of experience.

H: What? That's it? It seems that you are saying that knowledge equals experience only and I am sure that it does not, but I suspect that there may be a strong relationship between the two. I know that after I have experienced something I can say that I know it.

D: You are right. Knowledge is not precisely experience in its one dimension, but the assimilation of experience; knowledge is the establishment of the relationships between experiences; it is experience processing.

H: I'm afraid I do not follow you yet. I, first, need to ask you what an experience is.

D: Experience is the individual bits of impulses or stimuli.

H: How do you mean?

D: These impulses are of two types: exterior originating impulses such as sound waves, photons, heat, cold, or any other stimuli that we sense and register on our memory, and the interior originating experiences that come to our consciousness from within our corporate selves such as anger, fear, love, hurt, pain, pleasure and all the other emotions, feelings, and things that come to us from within.

H: OK.

D: The act of an interior or exterior originating stimulus pinging on the consciousness is a unit of experience. This bit of experience may be retained in memory or forgotten.

H: You mentioned "exterior originating impulses." I assume by "exterior originating" that you meant the same thing that we talked about when we discussed the nature of aesthetics which I have since put down in written form.

D: Yes.

H: And to summarize what we said was that "exterior originating" meant those stimuli that came to us from without and "interior originating" meant that which came to us from within our body or mind or even soul if you will.

D: Yes.

H: So when my consciousness registers and retains that it is hot in here, the act of sensing the heat is a bit of experience.

D: Yes. It is just as a computer does when you impute through its keyboard some number for a database or letters that form a word in a word processing document. The stimulus is entered and retained in memory, but nothing else has happened.

H: Is there any difference in the two examples you just mentioned, that is, the exterior originating impulses coming to the consciousness and the impulses being sent into a computer? In other words, you have freely related computers with consciousness and experience. Is this significant? Does it matter? Why not have said that information is the impulses coming to a recorder of one kind such as a tape recorder, computer, or other memory retentive machines?   Also, does experience have to come to the consciousness?   Is there a special relationship between consciousness and experience?

D: Whoa. One question at a time. First, the consciousness is where experiences are realized and where we get our identity and know who we are. This was made clear by Descartes in his Meditations.

H: Yes, true. I suppose lower forms of life experience things in their consciousness; it is just that they may not be aware of as many experiences as we have, especially the internally originating ones.

D: And not as many experiences are placed in memory as in humans; that is, they are not capable of taking in as much information as we do.

H: Wait.   Is there any difference between experience and information?

D: Only in that when experience is placed in memory, it becomes information.

H: And so when the consciousness takes in stimuli, as long as it is in memory, it is information. This concept seems to say that as the length of time or usage of the experiences lives in our consciousness or memory, the experiencesbecome informational which means that all experience is information of some sort or another. Can an organism experience something that is not a piece of information?

D: The criteria to judge information is how relevant the experience is to one's self. In essence, information is the value that the self puts on the importance of the individual experience that is incoming at the time. If the incoming stimulus is very important, it is noted, collated, used with other experiences, and cast into memory for future reference to order one's life and help insure its immediate and future survival.

H: So, information is experience that an organism deems important to itself in its effort to survive and live and thusly casts it into memory.

D: Yes.

H: So can there be any experiences that are not informational?

D: If the experience has no relevance to the organism's life, then the experience is not informational. This circumstance where the experience is totally valueless would be rare because organisms seek or wait for survival-oriented experiences, and should totally irrelevant information come to an organism, as soon as the organism recognizes that this experience has no pertinency to it, it will most likely discard the experience. But as I mentioned, this circumstance would be rare because the organism is always taking in stimuli from its environs, and it is necessary for any organism to know what is going on around it. As these experiences come to it, it will sort them out and place an order of priority to them all based on the classification or criteria of how important the experience is to its life.

H: I see. It appears that most experiences have some relevancy to an organism at least to some degree however minor, and the degree to which they are informational depends on how important they are to one's life.

D: Yes.

H: But I gather that even if one bit of experience is not as important as compared to another bit of experience, we call both experiences information even though one is more relevant to one's life.

D: Yes.

H: Then information is not really a graduated scale. All experience really needs to be classified as information is just at least a little bit of relevancy to somebody's life. If it has relevancy to anybody's life, then it is a bit of information and qualifies to be called information. It seems that we do not need to judge how relevant, only that it is relevant because just the fact that it is relevant qualifies the experience as information to someone.

D: It is true that once a bit of experience becomes relevant or important to at least some degree it takes on some value to life and becomes information.

H: Yes. I see. Can there be an experience that is not information?

D: An indication of the importance of a piece of information is the placement of it into long-term memory. When an experience occurs and the incoming stimulus disappears from our conscious memory, the term of its status as information approaches zero, and once out of memory, it looses such status altogether as we cast off selectively those bits of experience that are not important to us, or secondarily, to others.

H: Are you saying that as the duration of the experience in our conscious memory becomes smaller, the less it is informational?

D: Yes. And the more and longer it is placed in memory, the more it fulfills the essence of being informational.

H: So, I suspect that "memory" is needed to derive the standard of information. It seems that information must be in at least short-term memory and it would be better if it were in long term.

D: The definition of information is experience put in memory and the reason for it staying in memory is that it is relevant to the survival and well-being of an organism. The nature of experience is those stimuli that come to the consciousness.

H: OK.

D: Further, information is like any other term; it has a degree by which its nature is fulfilled.

H: I don't understand.

D: The terms by which we qualify the noun, or any highly conceptual word, will indicate a fulfillment of its essence. The most irrelevant piece of information to the existence and survival of you and me, such as how many steps there are to the stairs to this office or any other such piece of trivia, could be noted as useless information. But it is nevertheless information because we do have to climb the steps to get here. Although it does not matter to us what the exact number is, we know that there are individual steps, that there are a number of steps, that they have to be climbed, and that it is important to climb them to get here. We know from our experience that this is true and that this is somewhat important in our lives when we want to meet and discuss things and have to climb some stairs to meet someone to accomplish that purpose. But counting the individual number of steps would be out of the question. However, if someone walked in the door and announced it to us, we would probably note it, and after a short while it would pass from our memory because it is not important to us. And when it passes from memory, it no longer is information; the information no longer is in existence.

H: So if it is totally useless, then it would not be information, yet we have deemed it "useless information."

D: If it is truly, totally useless, then it is not information. It would be just an experience. However, when it comes to something like the number of steps there are to come up here, we deem it useless information because it is in all probability useless to us; and I say "in all probability" because we will most likely not be able to use this information in our lives because we will not be a construction contractor or architect who could be asked for the number of steps if this building were debilitating and needed to be rebuilt. This number of steps might be important information, therefore, it is called information because it is relevant to their profession. The architect who built this place would say that the number of steps were important to architectural plans and drawings. If there is relevancy to someone, then it is information because it will be probably retained in memory somewhere, somehow.

H: I see. But still, my question stands: if there is information that is not important to anyone, is it still information just as much as very important relevant experiences are in memory?

D: It is a matter of those experiences that fulfill the standard of that which is information in its fullest sense of the concept: just as there are some pictures that are more artistic than others, just as there are some authors that have produced the greatest novels such as Dickens and Hardy and many others, just as there are musical composers who are known as greater artists than others as their music is more appreciated, just as some things are more beautiful than other things, there are degrees to all conceptual terms, and information is no different.

H: I see. I suppose that this would be the cause for the term "important information" or "critical piece of information."

D: The more an experience is relevant or even critical to our survival, health, happiness, et cetera, the more it fulfills the concept of being information. And as the information becomes relevant to others throughout the world for the world's general well-being, the more the experience becomes important information not to be lost or discarded, and the more those stimuli that come to the consciousness and/or memory are relevant to well being, the more the concept of information will include the capacity of memory.

H: Why did you say that information is that stimuli that come to the "consciousness and/or memory?"

D: It is because information exists if it is presently being used in the consciousness and it exists if the self decides that this information is relevant to the self's well-being over time and should be kept in memory for recall at an appropriate time.

H: So long as information is available to the self, it does not matter where it is; it can be in the consciousness or in memory or in extended memory perhaps in a computer, a book, a tape recorder, or wherever.

D: Correct.

H: And hence, there are three components to information: the impulse, the relevancy to survival or well-being, and retention. While it is retained it is information; when it leaves retention, it is lost.

D: Good.

H: You mentioned the word "conceptual." I once heard that a professor explained that knowledge is a collection of concepts, and now that I think about it, I would say that knowledge is language or communication of any sort because language is just a collection of words and all words have a concept about them.

D: He would be essentially correct because a concept is a categorization of experiences, and concrete concepts are categorizing exterior originating experiences and emotive subjective concepts are those of the interior originating type. And this would make up parameter one, that is, the individual words of language, and the second parameter would be the composition of the individual word concepts being put together beside each other making phrases and sentences.

H: OK.   Back to the difference between information and experience.

D: Yes. Experience is the one-dimensional impression upon the consciousness.

H: What? I thought that was information. Am I wrong that I thought they would be different? You said that information was stimuli coming to the consciousness.

D: The difference is that information is the retention of events anywhere and experience is the impression of an event on the consciousness of a life; information is the personal retention of an event: it is the personal retention of something existent with any attendant action.

H: You mean that the only difference is that experience is stimuli that come to us personally; it becomes information when it is retained which would mean, I guess, that all information is experience. Is that right? Can there be no information that is not experience? It seems odd: what about the experience of pain? Is it information?

D: Yes, it is. You are being informed that something is wrong, and yes, all information is of experience and all experience is information as long as it is retained. If the experience falls from memory the essence of the experience is lost and ceases to be. Information, when it comes to a living entity, is an experience to that living entity and all experience that occurs to any living entity is of the nature of information as long as there is memory. The shorter the memory, the shorter is the existence of the information, and also the quicker the experience itself is lost.

H: Yes, I see that all experiences are events of one sort or another, and hence, I can see that information that comes to us personally would be experience.

D: And information that is retained somewhere else such as in a library or computer would be potential experience. If we go and retrieve information that resides not within us, then as soon as that information comes to us, it becomes an experience of itself.

H: What about those experiences or information that come from within such as something we discovered by thought?

D: There is no difference; it is just an interior-originating experience, and hence, it is totally informational in nature. The interior originating experience is a personal event and its occurrence is informational as long as we remember it.

H: I see. You said just a minute ago that information "is the personal retention of something existent with any attendant action." It seems from that statement that the "attendant action" does not have to be with the existence of something whereas it was my understanding that an event was existence plus action.

D: That's correct. And the informational event is the action of life's memory receptacle concerning the event.

H: Wait. You just said information is the recording of an event which is existence plus an action. But I thought that information was experience, relevancy, and retention. How do you correlate the two or can you?

D: Experience is the perception of the event; the relevancy is the decision to record the event and the retention is, obviously, the placement of the event in one's own memory, and then sometimes we record this information on to paper or put it in a computer for storage for access when needed by either ourselves or someone else.

H: It seems that information is non-human specific and it can stand alone without or outside of life. As long as it can be stored or retained, then can it be information?

D: Yes, the recording of an occurrence of an event (which implies that this can be accessed) and the makeup of this event which is existence plus action is information. Hence, information can stand separately from us, be retained somewhere, as in a computer, and be accessed by someone somewhere.

H: OK. It looks like we are finally coming to a starting point, an essence, or a building block from which we can work. As I understand it, information is the recording of an event and an event is the existence of something plus its movement.

D: Yes. That's right, experience being the conscious reception of an event.

H: But what if we record the existence of something without any movement or action attendant to that something? Let's say we discover the existence of a rock in a yard. It's not moving but we discovered it and have known about it, and we have information of its existence.

D: Our discovery of the rock is an event because there is an action of our opening our eyes, receiving impulses from without, seeing the rock, recognizing that there is a rock. In total, our discovering that a rock is before us is an event. Thinking of the rock is an action and the occurrence or formation of information and its retention in memory is an action in itself.

H: Well, I am not sure I understand this correctly. Let's say an astronomer finds a new something in space by either looking at it, or better yet, he cannot see it but knows it to be there because there are other telltale signs, such as light being bent in the area, and he reasons that there is a mass in the vicinity whose gravitational pull is influencing the paths of light, and so, concludes a mass is positioned there, but it is just that we cannot see it.

D: Yes.

H: Well, it does not seem that the existence of the mass is an event. The astronomer predicts it, and it may even be that this mass exists, but the fact that the mass exists does not indicate an event. The existence of a mass or the plain existence of anything is not an event, and our having information on its existence or probable existence is not an event.

D: I agree that the bare existence of something does not mean there is an event attendant to it. However, if, from the existence of something, something informational is generated, then an event has occurred in which the thing that exists is involved. For example, your mass in outer space was bending light, and because of our astronomer's action of detecting the bent light, he was able to induce the probable existence of a mass in a certain position. These actions have generated information about the mass and this information is retained in his brain and probably on paper and in computers and in other peoples 'brains the processes themselves all being events themselves, and whenever any of these events are recorded, they become information as long as they remain recorded somewhere. And when stimuli are recorded, information becomes existent and the generation of this information is an event.

H: Yes, but you said "with any attendant action" meaning that there should be some attendant action with the thing that exists. Therefore, I am wondering if the informational event can occur about something that is existing but without any attendant action, such as a rock in some woods. The existence of the rock is without any attendant action and therefore not an event. I am purporting here that information can be had of something that is not an event, but just of existence itself. What do you think, Detmar?

D: Information cannot happen without the action. Information can only happen when there is life to receive it. Information can only exist when there is the relevancy of life. Even if the object of the information, such as our rock, is not moving, we must do something to receive the information that it is there. At least one must open his eyes, then we do have the event of noticing the rock in front of us.

H: OK, I will agree that it seems that the receiving of information is an event, but what about this example: if we look at a geological formation, we can see that there are strata that indicate the various ages of its formation, and we can note the different types of rock such as igneous or metamorphic; the point is that we can glean certain information and yet no one was around at the time; the information was recorded in the strata and it exists without any attendant actions.

D: Yes, you have seemingly met all the criteria: that is, there is an event which is the formation of the rock, albeit slowly over many years, and a record set in the geologic strata. But the record of the geological strata is not a memory. The memory must be of life or life's extensions.

H: Sorry, I don't follow you.

D: Memory is life-specific. A record of geological strata is not memory until the facts reach one of life's memories however small, however short.

H: I don't see that there is any difference between geological strata or what is recorded in a book or computer.

D: The difference is that the book and computer are life's memory extensions made on purpose by life to extend its memory retention capabilities and it is selective about it. That is, life chooses which information it should take in and put in memory. The rest of the incoming data may be cast aside, not recognized and not memorized, lost, or discarded.

H: Okay, we choose selectively the information that we keep.

D: The purpose of all information is for survival of the organism. All living creatures carry information within them - at the very least in their genetic codes - and can accept at least some information from exterior originating experiences.

H: Is that the entire purpose of information - for survival?

D: Yes, and to further survival - to get as far away from misery as an organism can possibly get.

H: And information promotes this?

D: Yes. The organism selects what information is important to it; the rest it may discard. It puts this selected information into memory or as much as it can, for use in promoting its well-being which includes the capacity to proliferate.

Chapter Two

Knowledge

H: Let's get back to something interesting that we mentioned briefly near the opening of this conversation.

D: OK. What was that?

H: You said that knowledge was the assimilation of experience. What did you mean by that or specifically what did you mean by "assimilation?"

D: Experience is a one-dimensional impression on the consciousness; knowledge is establishing the relationship between the separate experiences or separate bits of information, and we do this in the arena of the consciousness by our interior originating experiences, mostly by the ones known as our thought processes.

H: I don't see why an individual piece of information cannot be a piece of knowledge, and for that matter why should a few individual experiences that have been assimilated not be a new piece of information? For example, can we not say that we have knowledge that the rock exists or can we not have knowledge of a bit of information? It seems to me that they are the same.

D: I suppose we could extend our definition of knowledge to include the individual bits of stimuli that come to us. But in all practicality, we do not use the term "knowledge" in such a way.

H: How so?

D: As the information coming to us becomes more varied, profuse, intricate, and involved, we correlate, relate, compare, contrast, analyze by using our logic and rationality to understand it all; knowledge is formed. We rarely use knowledge when referring to simple bits of information, but the more complicated the subject matter, the more our internal rationality is required to sort the incoming stimuli, and as the rationality manufactures an understanding of that which is around us, the more we tend to call these understandings knowledge.

H: Let's see. The more complicated the information becomes, the more we must apply our rationality to the incoming information to get an understanding which I assume is the same as knowledge.

D: Yes.

H: So if there are two bits of information that come to us and we apply a bit of rationality, is it that we get a bit of knowledge?

D: We use our thought faculties to take the individual bits of information and establish a relationship between the two. If our new understanding is confirmed by experience, then we would call the new conclusion, knowledge.

H: I am still unsure about the difference between knowledge and information because although I understand information to be the incoming stimuli to which we acknowledge relevancy and throw into memory and knowledge to be our internal rational capabilities, which are internally originating experiences, working on the information, I am convinced that this newly formulated knowledge is also informational, and hence, the distinction between the two concepts remains unclear.

D: As the newly formed knowledge becomes mature and we come to recognize it as familiar and understand it completely, it looses its lofty station as knowledge and becomes to be seen more as informational.

H: How so?

D: So far we have advanced the standard of knowledge to be that which is assimilated information.   Well, as we take in the stimuli and form new knowledge, we again use this established knowledge with other information or knowledge to form new knowledge pyramiding and building our wealth of knowledge. As we get farther from the original bits of information that are the base of this pyramid of information and knowledge, we note this knowledge at the top to be higher knowledge and the understandings toward the base to be just information or common knowledge. The lower in the pyramid of knowledge we go, we tend to label the understandings as information, common knowledge, or facts, but the higher we go, that is, the more we assimilate toward new or advanced knowledge the more we tend to label the higher or new understandings, "knowledge," especially "higher knowledge."

H: Then, as I understand it, we assimilate information to come up with or discover this new knowledge from previous knowledge, information, facts, or whatever which are all in the realm of information. Can there be knowledge that is not information?

D: No. As you perceived it, all knowledge and facts are within the realm of information.   We distinguish knowledge from information only as it becomes more complicated and becomes the pinnacle of that which we know.   For this higher form of information, we tend to designate it as "knowledge."

H: OK. But we have said that knowledge is the result of the assimilation of information. What do you mean by this?

D: Assimilating information is the application of our rational capacity to formulate new knowledge.

H: Well, what are these rational capacities? How is it that we are able to formulate new knowledge? What is the process?

D: Assimilation indicates the rational faculties of the consciousness which includes inductive and deductive logic, memory impute, memory recall, and will.

H: I am well aware of the capacities of memory recall, inductive, and deductive logic, but why do you include will, and how all this works together in order for us to create new knowledge is unclear.

D: First, there must be a will or an incentive to assimilate the information for whatever reason which will provide the inertia to become reactive and create knowledge. The information will come in, whether it is new or not, we combine it with information from memory, and reasoning is applied to create further knowledge.

H: How about an example of the creation of some knowledge?

D: If you are in a house without a jacket on and it is cold outside, our experience tells us that being inside protects us from the wind and cold outside. But after a while we begin to get hungry and decide that we need to get some food and the only way to get food is to go somewhere for it - introducing the will to the problem - and hence, we must go outside for the food where it is cold. Experience has taught us that the walls of our domicile protect us from the outside cold. We also have information that food is waiting for us in a different location. We have a problem to surmount which is how to get to the food without getting cold. In order to solve this problem we open our memory for examination by our capacity to reason inductively. We scroll through our memory examining items that may act as a portable miniature wall that we can use to protect our bodies from the outside elements. As our memory goes over information that there is some cloth or leather available, we inductively reason or extrapolate that we could employ the cloth or leather to the same purpose that we use the walls to our domicile except this new material would be portable. This extrapolation of the bits of memory information to predict the possibility of using the cloth or leather as a portable wall becomes a reality when we put it to the test and experience tells us that it works. At that point, we have discovered a new bit of knowledge which is that cloth and leather are valuable as protection against the weather and can be used for such purposes.

H: Is all knowledge created as such? Or are there other ways it can be created?

D: Yes, all knowledge uses these steps of the will, the memory, and the rationality applied to information to create knowledge.

H: It seems to me that the purpose of knowledge and information is to understand the world. Do you agree with this?

D: Yes, in general. But more precisely knowledge is used by the will in the arena of the consciousness to make decisions so that we may live as we want.

H: If the purpose of the will is to make decisions in life, then what is the nature of a decision?

D: All decisions are made when action (physical or mental) is required. When it comes to a point where we must do something in our lives such as to go to the store to get food or any other thing we may consider, a decision is required. In order to make this decision information comes to us informing us an action will be needed; when all the information is received from current events and from memory, usually there are a number of types of actions or possible alternatives to the problem of action that one may employ to consummate the action; that is, we may do one of several things to solve the problems of action. To these alternatives, we assign preferences or priorities that are based on the individual's personal understanding of what Aristotle would call "the good."

H: And what would be the essence of what "the good" is? How do we determine what is "the good" for an individual decision-maker?

D: If you will recall our conversation on ethics, we encountered this problem of the good. The good, or that which has virtue, is that behavior that first enables the individual to survive and secondly, that which enables those with whom he is socially entwined to survive and flourish, proliferate and become happy and experience that which pleases them and takes them further from the reaches of misery.

H: Yes, thank you for reminding me. I now recall that. But back to the problem of the assignment of priorities in making a decision. As I understand it, we are able to assign a preference to all alternatives when faced with a decision to make by an innate understanding of that which is good in relation to an individual's predicament.

D: Yes. We know basically from our interior originating experiences what is good for us and this understanding of the good enables us to assign priorities to the various alternatives and possibilities by which we may choose an action to solve a problem.

H: You seem to indicate that the good is relevant to only actions. You stated that the good is behavior that leads to survival which makes it life-specific. Cannot things be good also?

D: Yes. Things can be declared good or bad according to how well the thing is useful in promoting life and specifically the individual's life and the life of those around him. If the thing such as a house is considered, it is thought to be good because it harbors and protects us from the elements and gives us a place by which we may eat, live, and raise a family. A tree is good because it can provide wood and so on.

H: Now, allow me to change the subject slightly because I understand, I believe, your explanation of knowledge. I would like to return to my original question that opened this discussion.

Chapter Three

Truth

D: All right.

H: I asked how do we know something for sure; or how is it that we know something is true? What is truth?

D: Truth is knowledge without inconsistency.

H: Well, of course, knowledge is without inconsistency. Knowledge could not be knowledge if there were an inconsistency. I would say that by definition knowledge itself appears to be true. It just seems that the standard of that which is true should not contain the word knowledge because it contains the sense of truth within it.

D: Yes. I understand your point so we will say that truth is experience that we commit to memory that is without inconsistency relative to our other experiences.

H: Can you elaborate a bit? I think I see where you are going.

D: We mentioned a bit ago our pyramid of knowledge. We have sought to understand the world, and to do so, we have built up our fund of knowledge by assimilating experience. As we assimilate experience, we endeavor to avoid mistakes in the application of our rationality to the experiences in building our knowledge. And as we refine our knowledge and eliminate inconsistencies, we approach truth. And, of course, when we have eliminated all inconsistencies from our experiences we have truth.

H: This sounds a little like William James in his essay on truth.

D: Yes, truth is essentially, as he noted, that which "we can assimilate, validate, corroborate, and verify."

H: But sometimes we can have knowledge and yet it may not be true. For example, Newton's laws as it turns out were not quite right. They seemed to be right, but Einstein later showed that they were not quite accurate and came up with new equations that enabled physicists to be more precise, yet we still say that we have knowledge of Newton's equations and Newtonian physics.

D: Yes, Newton's physics are knowledge and they are true.

H: But there is the inconsistency of the equations not being complete and totally accurate.

D: Newton's physics is complete in itself without inconsistency as for as it goes, and it is useful to a point and certainly it is useful consistent knowledge for everyday life.

H: But it has an inconsistency. I do not follow you.

D: Actually, there is no inconsistency; it is a matter of completeness and more importantly, relevancy.

H: How so?

D: The Newtonian equations are correct and true and without inconsistency as for as they go. Your point is that they do not go further to cover the problems of accuracy. As we approach high speed, the Newtonian equations are not accurate, and therefore there is an inherent inconsistency. But the real problem is its degree of relevancy to problems that are not at high speed. They are correct as for as they go. And the same thing goes for the Einstein equations: they are more relevant but not completely absolutely relevant.

H: I do not understand your usage of relevancy. Relevancy to what? And how can something be "absolutely relevant?"

D: In the same sense that we have been using relevancy at other times throughout our discourse. Relevancy means a frame of reference and absolute relevancy means that the frame of reference covers all circumstances and situations. A frame of reference that we have been referring to is Aristotle's "good." And the good is that which promotes living. The better something is for the advancement of life, the more relevant it is to our purposes of living, as life is the most important aspect conceivable to us. There is nothing more important to life than its survival. The more propitious circumstances are to favor life, the more these circumstances are relevant to our being. The good is that which favors life.

H: Can you tie the good, relevancy, truth, and why Newtonian equations are not inconsistent together?

D: As iterated, the good is that which promotes life. The more we insure our survival by producing goods and services that take us further from bare, mean, survival and give us a margin from death, the better we are off and the more it is good. Relevancy is for whom the good is.

H: Wait a second. Do I understand you correctly in that relevancy means that there must be good for somebody and that truth and knowledge must have a relevancy to somebody which would mean that if there is nobody to whom the good has relevancy, then truth cannot exist? It seems that you have said that truth is relevant to that which is good. But I am sure then that it can be relevant to the bad and that there can be bad truth.

D: The purpose of knowledge and the existence of truth is for the good. Mankind's building of knowledge is good. Yes, there are times when there is information that is about bad things, but the capacity to get and receive information to create and further our knowledge is good. We need knowledge in order to better our predicament. The more knowledge the more we insure our survival and hence the more we have the good.

H: But what about when bad or evil people get hold of knowledge that they can use to do bad things? Bad men could create knowledge for bad purposes.

D: Sometimes people are bad but the purpose of knowledge is to promote the good.

H: It seems that information and knowledge should be neutral and not necessarily good or bad.

D: All information and then knowledge must be for the ultimate purpose of survival. If there are bad people who are creating knowledge for destruction, they do it for ideological purposes whose tenets are purporting some sort of utopia that, they believe, is ultimately good for somebody even though it may seem irrational. I suppose that there could be somebody so evil that all he aims for is the total destruction of all life which would be for his own personal self-destruction as well. But throughout nature, this situation seems highly improbable. This is not to say that it is impossible because an anomaly can always pop up. But the general purpose of knowledge through nature is to promote self-survival, and self-survival promotes social survival when it is seen that cooperation amongst individuals promotes self-survival as well as group survival. I think we went into detail about this when we discussed the nature of ethics.

H: OK. I agree that overall knowledge is for the good, and the good is based on survival. Let's go to relevancy. How does this fit into this scheme?

D: All knowledge must be relevant to something living as only the living can hold knowledge. And since all knowledge resides in something living (or in its extra-memory tool), any system of knowledge will begin with the living entity. So when we say that a bit of information, knowledge, or some Newtonian equations has relevancy, we mean that this knowledge emanated from a previous system of thought that has been developed to negotiate a set of problems and determine solutions as to what to do in one's life - to encounter experience, assimilate it, and decide how to live.

H: I am beginning to see what you are talking about. Let's get back to the Newtonian physics: what is the relevancy of the equations; why are they true and belong to truth even though they are not complete truth?

D: Because Newton devised them to explain the universe as he experienced it - as he saw it - and his explanation worked without inconsistencies because his experiences were limited, and hence, his equations were true to the relevancy of his experiences. Experience is the basic component of information; it is the raw material by which, first, all information is composed, and then, when mixed with our internal experiences, becomes knowledge. Life possesses all knowledge; no knowledge can be outside of life's control.

H: You are referring to our ability to externalize information in books, computers, et cetera.

D: Yes. Knowledge and information exist either in life or in a life-controlled or life-recognized receptacle of storage. Life uses this information and knowledge to negotiate its daily problems and make decisions that enable it to survive and improve itself and keep itself as far away from misery and death as possible. The whole purpose of information is to let life live and survive as well as possible.

H: OK.

D: And in order to live, life must act; it cannot be completely passive; it must get and process food at the very least. As the more complicated the life form is, the more the action, travail, effort, energy it must use, and generally the more complicated its predicament becomes. In any case, whatever life form it is, some action is required to negotiate its predicaments and this requires a decision. The decision arises when information - nay, experiences - demonstrates to the consciousness that something must be done for whatever reason in order to live. For example, when the organism becomes hungry, information comes to the consciousness that tells it of this condition and a choice must be made at least to the extent of whether to proceed with the acquisition of food or not, and if so, the organism will consider how to do it, that is, an action will be required, a decision made. The organism in order to decide anything will appoint a priority to its available choices. These priorities emerge as internal experiences themselves and are comprised of our rational and emotional experiences. The consciousness uses these rationalities and emotions to assign priorities - a kind of knowledge - to the available choice of actions that are needed to live, survive, and hopefully, survive well without much misery. These priorities that are assigned by the individual are based in the good that will proceed from the decided actions.

H: Could you go over that process once more?

D: Experiences come to the individual that inform it that it must do an action should it want to satisfy a desire. The individual will use internal originating experiences of rationality and emotions to assign its priorities to the available possibilities. The rational faculties, emotions, and other human mental capacities use the scale of the good as its yardstick to assign its priorities. This good is that which is realized by the rationalities as that which will promote survival, life, and keep the individual as far away from misery as possible. To summarize, the individual's physical makeup in combination with its environment produces a predicament where a decision is needed. The individual's internal workings realize through its learned knowledge and information what is good or best for it. The alternatives available in the predicament are assigned the degree of good from which is established the priority, and the action (or non-action) is decided and commenced.

H: I see. And truth, relevancy, and the good?

D: To make life's decisions, information and knowledge are collected, expanded, and stored, and made available for reference when making its priorities of the good. Without this library of knowledge, the individual cannot make an informed decision or the best decision available to him. And, of course, in order to make good decisions the information needs to be without mistakes, contradictions, or incongruities. That is, one bit of information should not be contradictory to another.

H: Yes, this is a basic law of logic.

D: When information and knowledge are built by one or many individuals, the information becomes valid and true when all inconsistencies are eliminated.

H: Well, what about the problem of Newton again, or where may the system of knowledge be incomplete?

D: If it works to make decisions for the good, it will remain true despite the problem of incompleteness because it operates without inconsistencies to allow the individual to make decisions that are good and promote survival, and decrease misery.

H: So it seems that knowledge is true if it produces decision making which is to the good.

D: Yes, that is correct.

H: But it seems to me that the good is totally subjective. For one person's good is different from another's, and further; it seems that this reasoning would soon be - or actually, has been - readily used by politicos overly empowered by the state purporting that the truth is that which will facilitate the state in providing all that is good for the people and whatever information that helps the state to this end will be written so and declared true no matter if it really happened or not: truth will be that which is construed by the state for its own good purposes.

D: I see your point.

H: And what if the information is held by an unethical or even evil person? The information and knowledge will most likely be used for the unethical, not virtuous, and the no good.

D: First, information is used by life for the sake of life in general and that is good, and ultimately the purpose of all information is to promote the furtherance of life which is the criteria of the good. But, as you say, there are problems of the unethical and especially the evil where unethical behavior is combined with an unethical objective as you expounded in your manuscript on ethics. One of your objections is when information and knowledge fall into the hands of the bad and this information is exploited for the bad's bad purposes (which would be evil).

H: Yes.

D: We touched upon this earlier a bit, but when this happens, it is an exception. When information is used by the evil for its bad purposes, it does not invalidate our statement that knowledge is for the use of life to survive. It still remains that this still happens; it is just that in the midst of life there emerges an aberration where an individual appears with his unethical objectives, tries to obtain them, and in doing so causes misery and death. The origins of this evil, as we mentioned in a previous discussion of ethics, probably have its beginnings in pure selfishness. It appears that the good is somehow corrupted by selfishness or possibly by an aberration or a mistake in genetic information which occasionally happens.   As noted previously in your tome on ethics, the world of life in the universe is run by an admixture of free will, risk, time, information/knowledge, and effort which make up our sacrifices that we perform to carry on our lives. And we know that because where there is free will, there is risk, and when there is risk, there are times when all will not be successful even in the creation of individuals in life, as some may be beset with faulty genetic information or some may react to their environment in an anti-social way. And if life were to produce evil on a regular basis, life, or at least human life, would not prosper and develop has it has. It would head for eventual extinction.

H: But somehow I am not satisfied with this answer.

D: If for some reason an individual lives a life of evil such as a serial murderer, or a political murderer, the evil is a corruption of the good. Evil does not appear separately as a distinct entity. Because the individual always holds from their inception the desire of self-survival, the evil one occasionally may misunderstand or misapply ideology; the list is endless of what may go wrong in the universe due to the presence of risk and free will.

H: Yes, I remember in our inquiry into the nature of ethics the discussion of this problem. I see that life works toward the good and it needs information to this end. And because of the risk of being alive in a universe where the free will of the individual life entity reigns throughout its daily life, things can go wrong, but the wrong is without the intent of life to be that way as life worked for its own promotion which is the basis of the good.

D: Correct.

H: OK.   Let's get back to the question of the good being subjective. You mentioned that knowledge works to make decisions to the good and we now would like to accept that, but if we do, it seems that since good appears to be mostly a subjective standard, it would imply that truth is also subjective, and hence it would be hard to say that one is wrong when working toward something that they deem as good.

D: The relationship between good and truth is that consistent knowledge is truth and it is good for life, therefore, knowledge is good and truth is good.

H: But good is a subjective thing. Truth should be objective.

D: First, we should point out that truth and knowledge are of the good. We need consistent knowledge to advance and make progress in this world, to bring mankind up away from misery to a better and good life.   Secondly, the good is not a subjective notion; it is objective.   We have stated what good is and when something conforms to that standard, then we can know that that thing is good.

H: Yes, we stated that the good is that which promotes and furthers the survival of life first for the individual and secondly for the society of the individual and all those with whom we come in contact and cooperate.

D: Yes, that is the standard of the good and so anything that does not comply with that standard will not be good and everything that does will be of the good and the more something promotes life, the more it is good. The greater something is good, the greater is its life promotion factor.

H: I see. So we can say that good is objective, but can we know if there is absolute good, or for that matter, absolute truth or absolute knowledge? Is there such a thing?

D: If you mean do we know everything, then no, we have not achieved that obviously.   If you mean whether some of the knowledge that we presently possess is absolute or perfect in itself or as far as it goes, then yes some of our knowledge is absolute. That is, some of it is truly and perfectly without any inconsistency or incongruity and is consistent in every extent. This is what Descartes demonstrated in his Meditations. He came up with some knowledge that was absolutely true to those who think. Every consciousness that thinks is aware of itself and hence, exists. So, yes, we can and do have absolute knowledge - something we can know for sure. But it is absolutely true within its realm of relevancy.   In this case, Descartes 'knowledge was true for life with consciousness.

H: Can we have frames of relevancy of knowledge where things become more complicated?

D: Certainly.   All you have to do is make sure you have eliminated the contradictions and inconsistencies.   This is done usually by peer review over time just as Newton was examined or any other producer of knowledge. Sometimes in more complicated nebulous areas, the review seems to never end; but the constant examination is healthy as slowly the inconsistencies come out of the systems of knowledge. Hence, sometimes we can and do discover absolutes, but we must remember the frame of reference of these absolute truths.   That is, they may be absolutely true within their frame of reference.

H: Again, we are back to this problem of the reference point or relevancy of truth. Please let's go over it again.

D: The frame of truth relevancy for Descartes 'first Meditation where he discovers his famous conclusion, which is also a starting point, is himself. He knows that this truth is perfect and absolute for him and that he has examined it completely and this bit of knowledge is without inconsistency and contradiction. This frame of relevancy widens when others examine it and are satisfied as to its efficacy and they also come to the same conclusion. And as more and more people read it, examine it, and search for inconsistencies, and adapt it to our library of knowledge, we use inductive logic to know that his conclusion and starting point is an universal truth for all living things that think. There are other bits of knowledge that are applicable to such great lengths to the universe.

H: Such as.

D: The theories of the four forces of the universe. They are applicable everywhere we look except possibly at the subatomic level where scientists look to find the unifying theory that can explain how all these four theories work together. These theories work out and explain things to satisfaction but scientists realize that they are close to being entirely absolute but not quite there. They are only absolute as far as their frames of relevancy go. They explain everything satisfactorily within these frames but the frames of relevancy are limited.

H: Your speaking of the theories of the four major forces which are gravity, strong nuclear forces, the weak atomic forces, and the electromagnetic forces. There is no expression that can tell us how these four different forces coexist and under what principle or principles they operate.

D: Yes. Gravity is everywhere and is an absolute truth up to the point where the problem of how it works and how it differs from the other forces of nature.

H: I see. So you are saying that truth is always absolute within its limiting parameters. Of course, some truths have greater limiting parameters than others.

D: Yes. In some areas, knowledge is very limited, but in others it is extensive, and as long as we take out the inconsistencies and contradictions, then within the limits of the knowledge, it is absolute within its frame of reference. We know how far Newtonian physics go, and we know for what problems it works, and within these limits of its frame of reference Newtonian physics are true and incontrovertible.

Chapter Four

Consciousness

H: You mentioned that there are four basic forces of nature - gravity, strong nuclear forces, weak atomic forces, and the electromagnetic forces. Do you think that they will find the unifying theory to explain it all?

D: I understand that they may find the next step shortly that may begin to explain the connection between the four forces, but I do not think that we could call it truly a unifying theory.

H: Why not?

D: Because there is at least one more force that is not included but just as prominent and that is the force of life that changes the most basic characteristics of atoms and molecules.

H: I don't follow you. What do you mean by life force?

D: I mean that life has a force within it that enables molecules to go from a state of entropy to one of an anti-entropic state, or to initiate a word for our own purposes, we might say "animatepomorphic," which is the basic characteristic of life.

H: It would seem you are right. There must be another force in the universe that causes life because life certainly does not behave according to the laws of physics. It, of course, is something separate and different, and it makes sense that it is, as you say, anti-entropic. I understand the law of thermodynamics which states that energy tends to seek equilibrium. And now that you mention it, life is the opposite; life stops this condition of entropy. How does it manage this?

D: It can only do so by the use of knowledge.

H: What? What do you mean?

D: When the first atom reversed itself from the entropic state and started to organize with other atoms, it could only move away from entropy and do something else if it knew what to do. That is, it must have had knowledge. The first signs of life had knowledge of some sort.

H: Well then, according to the definition of knowledge the original atom or atoms that reversed themselves out of the entropic state and went to the anti-entropic state did so by assimilation of information or by the assimilation of experience.

D: Yes, and not only that, but it used the information to do what all life does - it made a decision for the purpose of initiating an action.

H: All life makes decisions? How about a plant? They do not seem to me to make decisions; I would suppose that only the animal world makes actual decisions as they must have movement and actions in order to live.

D: So do plants, but it is limited. Plants germinate, grow roots, sprout, take in sunlight, manufacture nutrition, and grow. They are tropic as they also will decide to grow toward sunlight. Granted as a whole, they do not have much movement, but internally in each cell, they basically make all the decisions necessary to their lives.

H: So the basic characteristics of life are that it makes decisions and is anti-entropic?

D: In order for matter to be anti-entropic, it must make a decision, and to make decisions you need an arena where information is used to assign priorities of action.

H: That seems to me a characteristic again of the animal world. You are speaking of the consciousness of an organism which is of the animal world. It does not seem to me that this exists in the plant or cellular world.

D: Knowledge is present anywhere there is life and where there is life there are decisions, and in order to make a decision there is an arena of consciousness however slight and tiny.

H: How is it that a plant or a cell or even the first primitive sign of life has a consciousness?

D: Your idea of a consciousness is too grand. It is only where decisions are made. Your consciousness has long-term memory, short-term memory, rationality, and emotions coming to it enabling it to make decisions.

H: Still I do not see how consciousness can be present at the cellular level.

D: In order to be life, matter must act in an anti-entropic way. To act anti-entropically, life must act in making decisions. These decisions demonstrate life's anti-entropic characteristic. To make a decision knowledge is required. As an animal, this is plainly seen.

H: Yes. An animal will decide many things, and we can see that he acts as humans do in deciding to seek food, shelter, reproduce, et al. And obviously, an animal has at least a limited memory and decision-making process.

D: However, even lower forms of life will decide what to do in their lives. A cell will flagellate through water. This is an action. It could decide not to flagellate or flagellate, and this is a decision, and decisions are based on knowledge and information.

H: But, I still do not see that a basic ability to decide something extremely simple necessitates the conclusion that a single-celled organism has a consciousness.

D: A consciousness is the arena where information and knowledge are gathered and put against a set of already assimilated interior-originating experiences, which are the priorities, to make decisions. It is where experiences gather and rationality is applied to make decisions. The purpose of the consciousness is to make decisions so as to allow the organism to survive and reproduce and to allow the DNA to survive so as to perpetuate life.

H: I agree that at least higher organisms need the consciousness to survive. It seems that there is so much information about us that some sort of an arena is needed to process all of the information and knowledge.

D: Precisely. An arena is needed to process the information for the cells making up the organism. But it does not matter as to the degree of information or number of experiences coming to the organism. At the complicated level, it is easy to see that a consciousness is necessary for the organism to operate. We have only to look at ourselves to realize this. If we extrapolate the experiencing of our own consciousness to that of a lesser but yet complicated organism, we can readily see that our dog or cat has a consciousness.

H: Yes. It is when I consider the lesser organisms, such as an ant, or lesser yet, a single-celled organism.

D: Wherever a decision is made, the beginnings or rudiments of a consciousness necessarily appear. As consciousness is where experience is processed in order to make a decision, anywhere life's decisions are made, there exists a consciousness. The lesser the organism, the lesser the processing of information and the lesser the number of decisions; but as long as a decision is being made, a consciousness exists.

H: Even in an ant?

D: Yes. If you watch the ant come into your kitchen going this way or that looking, searching for food, he makes decisions. He makes the decision to go search for food, he decides on a direction by using his sensitivity to aromas, and hence he is able to find food and bring it back to the nest. Ants are successful in surviving, and they do this by taking in information and making decisions.

H: But information implies memory; that means they would have to have memory.

D: They do have some capacity for memory. Ants can remember where food lies and they come back for it. But experience becomes information as soon as it stays for any length of time: if it is long enough just to make a decision, experience becomes information; if after that, the information passes from memory, the information is lost and the consciousness is limited to that extent.

H: So actually, the greater the capacity to process information and keep it in memory and make decisions, the greater the consciousness.

D: Correct.

H: And with regard to the smallness of a one-celled organism or even to a plant, is there consciousness? It does not seem likely there is any place for the consciousness to exist. There is no brain or nerve center for the arena of the decision-making process to exist.

D: Yes, it exists even without a nerve center. Actually, all that is required is the existence of knowledge and a decision. Knowledge or information provides the raw material for the rationality in order to effect the decision, and a decision requires the conscious will to choose to do something.

H: This sounds like free will.

D: Yes. Free will is the opportunity to weigh information, to choose that which is most fitting for the organism, or to do what it needs to do in order to survive. If there were no free will, risk would devour it and life. Free will exists to combat the risk of the existence of life. Free will is the discretion by the entity to use its available information to survive in the face of a risky universe.

H: Let's get back to the smallness of life. How about the first appearance of life with regard to consciousness?

D: Consciousness existed the moment life appeared. That is, when the first molecule went from its state of entropy to the anti-entropic, a decision was made to execute this change of states which cannot happen randomly, and therefore, knowledge existed preparatory to the decision.

H: But the knowledge and the capacity to do so came from somewhere.

D: Of course, because at the inception of the anti-entropic state, that is, at this first step (since there was no antecedent and risk was everywhere) because there was no free will, no ability to decide, no consciousness or arena to decide, the first decision must have been divinely inspired. That is, it was not of free will that life could spring. At life's inception, there was no free will. Free will only exists once the anti-entropic state exists, but to initiate the anti-entropic condition from the state of entropy a decision where free will is absent is necessary.

H: And as we discussed in our conversation about ethics, life without free will has to be divine in nature to exist. Hence, the inception of life was divine.

D: Yes. Life is of divine origin because the original decision of the molecule or molecules to protect itself from the risk of existing in this universe is without free will. It was not by life's choice that life exists, and therefore life could not have just occurred in the seas and then evolved.

H: And so life has a creator?

D: Certainly yes. Without a doubt. Knowledge and free will were needed to take molecules from a state of entropy to the anti-entropic state of life.

H: You said just a little bit ago that the greater the capacity to process information, the greater the consciousness.

D: Yes.

H: And so to be all-knowing, the consciousness must have the capacity of handling and processing all the existing information. And if all information could be processed, could that all-knowing being that can do this processing eliminate risk and be perfect?

D: Should there be a consciousness perhaps divinatory in nature that is powerful enough to take in all information and process it completely and perfectly, it would be the greatest consciousness, but it would not eliminate the element of risk about it if anything exists outside of it. It could calculate probabilities perfectly to know always what is best overall for its survival. But risk is not eliminated for that which is anti-entropic. As long as there is matter, and energy with characteristics present such as the Uncertainty Principle of physics, risk will be present to life.

H: How about to the divine, the creator of life? Would he be subject to risk?

D: If he is of life, then his is subject to risk. If he is more than life, then maybe not.

H: How could he be more than life? What do you mean?

D: We spoke of the search of the unifying theory that will tie the four forces of the universe together.

H: Yes.

D: If we include a greater unifying theory that unifies the forces of the universe with the life force, we will find something greater than life. The knowledge that unifies life with matter and energy and the entropic universe will be greater than life. The creator, the father of life, will have this knowledge of the ultimate unifying theory and will be greater than life itself. And it will not only have the knowledge of the life force and the unifying theory of the four universal atomic forces, but the creator will have the ability to create and destroy all through his knowledge.

H: Let's get back to the point that you mentioned a while ago about consciousness being the arena where the individual weighs the various life experiences, i.e. information and knowledge, and makes its decision as to what to do with its life using the yardstick of the will to survive.

D: OK.

H: You have mentioned that the consciousness exists for the organism, but you have also stated that anywhere that life exists, or that is, anywhere a decision is made, there is life. And therefore, there is a consciousness at all levels of life even down to the single cell, even down to the moment and place when life started at its original inception or maybe even at its conception in another life body. I am wondering at the minute level, at the cellular or molecular level, whether this is the same type of consciousness as at the complicated stage of life. I am having a hard time assimilating the idea that a consciousness exists at the cellular, viral, or even molecular level.

D: The nature of consciousness is the discretion to use knowledge for a purpose; the purpose, of course, being its perpetuation and secondarily in its complicated stages to get as far away from misery and toward the good as possible.

H: Explain, please.

D: The process at the complicated level is the same as at the minute level; it is even the same at the cellular or molecular level. When matter uses knowledge for anti-entropic purposes, a consciousness exists. When the first molecule went anti-entropic and gathered and commandeered another molecule or stored or used other molecules for the purpose of protection from the surrounding environment, it had to use knowledge to make a decision in an arena where the knowledge convenes with the control energy, or the anti-entropic life force, to perform the action. This arena where knowledge convenes with energy is consciousness.

H: Consciousness is only knowledge convening with energy? I thought you said there was this standard of survival also.

D: Yes. But the standard of survival and perpetuation of life is a type or bit of knowledge. The standard is of the internal originating experiences of the organism except at the inception of life where this knowledge was injected into the molecule or molecules from the creator.

H: So, let's go over its nature again.

D: Consciousness is interior originating knowledge, free will, memory plus anti-entropic energy.

H: How's that? I understand "knowledge" and "memory" here, but what of this "anti-entropic energy?"

D: This anti-entropic energy is life's energy. It's composition is unknown to us mortals, and only to the father of life. This life energy can use knowledge at our level of existence to garner the existent available matter and energy to its own use in perpetuating itself and protecting itself from the environment. It needs to build a shield around itself for its perpetuation.

H: Why? Why does it need or want to? If this life energy with its attendant knowledge existed - which would make it necessarily have a consciousness - at a previous point in time, why should it want to suddenly garner molecules and energy and build itself a barrier to the rest of the world? Why did it want to change?

D: We can only speculate as to the nature of the creator's life force and his power over the universe. Perhaps, though, it is a good idea to go over what we have established. We know that consciousness consists of experience - in the form of information or knowledge, free will, and the life force.

H: If that is the case, then at the inception of life, as we mentioned before, a consciousness existed, and that all life must have at least a small consciousness.

D: Yes, and this life force that we allude to must have at least some knowledge with it because life must make decisions from its inception as life exists amidst a world of risk.

H: So, if life has its consciousness, that is, it has its life energy and knowledge, this implies that a memory, at least a short-term one, exists.

D: Yes. In order for life to exist it must have the rudiments of a memory of the knowledge that it takes to exist in this world of risk. All life must make at least some decisions and this takes a memory for the information that concerns the organism in its struggles to stay alive and proliferate, and if it cannot proliferate, it will die out completely as its environment will eventually, due to the existence of risk, destroy it.

H: Yes, I understand this and can agree with it. So all life has consciousness, even the single-celled, and it consists of this force or energy that can cause molecules to go to an anti-entropic state which can garner energy for itself through its possession of knowledge which lies in its memory. It seems that we could conclude from this that we do not exist without a consciousness. And it would seem that the gradation of the capacity of the consciousness to retain experiences and assimilate knowledge corresponds to our phrases I have heard in biology class referred to as "lower life forms" and "higher life forms." It would seem we might judge the importance of life by this gradation of the capacity of the consciousness.

D: Yes. Without consciousness we have nothing; we have death. It is our consciousness that is so important to us. We hope that upon death we, nay, our consciousness will be resurrected: we are not as concerned about our bodies; of course, the resurrection of our bodies would be nice too, but not necessary; because if we are conscious, we know we are alive as Descartes pointed out.

H: Yes. I agree. But we have established that consciousness contains our experiences which would mean that we would want to be resurrected with our experiences.

D: Good point. That is true. Without the memory of our collective experiences, the consciousness becomes nothing. As our memory of our experiences decreases, the capacity and expanse of consciousness decreases and hence our identity. If suddenly - let's say by amnesia - we lost our past memory, our identity goes to zero, and has to start over. The same would be if we died, were resurrected, and became conscious again in heaven without our former experiences in memory; we would be as if we had a new identity and not be aware that we existed in a former life. It would be that we never existed. The man with total amnesia would feel that he began existing at the point where his memory was again collecting and storing information.

H: Yes. I think I see your point. I remember my first memory of existence. It is probably around age three or possibly just a little bit before when I am walking, or actually, I was running before my father on the sidewalk back to the apartment my parents had at the time. It is my first recollection. And my feeling is almost as if I did not exist before that point. It is as if the whole history of the universe passed in an instant to the point where I had my first memory.

D: When you die, unless your consciousness is resurrected with its memory and at least some of its interior originating experiences in tact, the whole rest of the history of the universe will pass in an instant.

H: And essentially, I was dead to the point of the beginning of my consciousness which was in my mother's womb.

D: Yes. Interesting point. At that inception of consciousness you, of course, began living even though you were not able to develop a long-term cognitive memory yet, but you had memory available at least at the genetic level. Also, after being born the long-term memory began to develop and you began to remember experiences longer and longer. At first, as a baby your memory is short, so you are alive but it does not yet extend to adulthood consciousness where your identity becomes mature.

H: Yes. I see. It is our identity that we want to cause to continue and this is our collection of experiences. I suppose if we cannot have our consciousness continue to exist in this life or world, we do pass some of our internal originating experiences in the form of our physical and human behavioral characteristics through the information that is held at the genetic level.

D: Yes. Naturally, we pass our genetic information on to our progeny. We have information stored at the genetic level and at the conscious level, and we have concluded that there is a level of consciousness at all levels of life: wherever there are decisions made according to the standard of survival, we have consciousness, and as this decision-making process can happen at the cellular level, there can be consciousness or a life awareness at the cellular level and above.

H: So, it seems to me that when a group of cells gather together and coordinate their efforts to make an organism, there appears to be two separate consciousnesses - one at the individual cellular level and another at the individual organism level. It almost seems that there are two different consciousnesses to an individual organism. Yet, as an individual, I feel and am aware of only one - the part that thinks and gives me my identity - the one that tells me I am alive and here and experiencing, as Descartes limned.

D: Yes, and there may even be a third consciousness evolving presently in the form of artificial intelligence should such a thing be possible to achieve.

H: How so?

D: Life at the genetic cellular level knows that to be more successful it should organize, develop, and hold more information and knowledge to take life further away from bare existence, and in order to do this a separate consciousness is needed to perform the coordination of the cells and act for all the cells in making the decisions according to the standard of its group survival. This group consciousness supersedes the individual level for the sake of the group and this secondary consciousness superintends all the problems of the group as it deals with its environment.

H: Is this possible - to have two or more consciousnesses?

D: Of course, if you cut yourself or you get sick, the subconscious and individual cellular decision-makers address the problem and heal the cut or cure the sickness if it can. This problem does not come to the group consciousness level. Decisions to heal the body are made at the subconscious and cellular levels.

H: You mentioned a third consciousness perhaps emerging from the research on intelligence whereby a machine, computer, humanoid, or whatever can think for itself. There is a new term for this that has emerged which is artificial intelligence, a.k.a., A.I.

D: Yes. A tertiary consciousness seems to be emerging in the form of computer memory and abilities, but whether a true tertiary consciousness will develop with its own individual decision-making properties I cannot tell. But I will guess that we will not be able to create a truly intelligent computer that has the ability to make decisions for its own survival and well-being in mind. A decision-making ability requires the discretionary faculty that enables the individual entity to act according to the standard of the individual's desire to survive.

H: Well, that would mean that Hal would have been alive and had a consciousness?

D: If you mean the on board computer in 2001, then yes, he had a consciousness and was alive because he was making decisions discretionary to his own well-being and survival.

H: Well, you said that the individual cells decided to band together to develop more complicated beings so that there would be greater insurance of survival of the life force or energy. I am not convinced that life requires more complicated, greater information-holding organisms to exist in order to insure survival or take life farther away from the brink of extinction. For example, look at the success of single-celled life forms. Certainly we can say that the simple life forms are the most successful throughout the world. Look at plankton. It is throughout the oceans of the world and produces the oxygen by which the animal kingdom is able to respire. Is there a true need for life to become more complicated? I see where the plant world proliferated and stepped into the ecological niches that were available for it on land and in the sea. But I do not see the necessity for the animal kingdom to proliferate and develop just for the sake of the survival of life. It does not seem necessary in the total scheme of things: as a matter of fact, this brings me back to the question that started this series of questions of why life was started to begin with. Hence, why should it start in the first place, and secondarily, why should it continue to develop in size and especially why should it develop complicated organisms with extensive consciousnesses? I am aware of the evolutionary doctrine that life reproduces and moves into ecological niches in order to find and make a living, but is that all there is to it?

D: We know that the standard by which all things live and exist is to survive and that survival of life and the continuation of life is good. We also know that the individual does things, acts, and makes decisions for his own good, his own good being commensurate with not only his survival but how well be survives. The more good he can bring himself the better are his chances of survival which is indicated by his general level of happiness whatever this mixture of happiness ingredients is. But the more good, the greater is the survival coefficient and the greater is the potential to reproduce and proliferate insuring the potential to overall survival and the continuation of life, as the genetic information tells our consciousness through the interior originating experiences that life is important so the individual should work to insure its own survival and try to prosper so that further life may be ensured.

H: OK.

D: So we know that life is good, that to strive to ensure the existence of life is good, and, as we studied in our discourse on ethics, that the good is what is the basis for behavior of life.

H: Yes.

D: So the evolutionary theory indicates that life proliferates and finds new niches by which to expand and flourish and this spreading of life to new niches is good.

H: Definitely.

D: We now know that there is a creator of life, and he has the knowledge and power over the ultimate unifying force. That is, he knows how matter and energy are interactive, how gravity and the other atomic forces and the life force are compatible, and how they exist together. We know further that the stark act of creating life is good.

H: You are assuming that.

D: No. I know it for sure. The creator initiating life here on earth is of the good as it is true for life to do good. We are to strive to do good and therefore the initiation of life itself was a good act. We further know that the creator's existence itself and his production of life are of the good. His existence and our subsequent existence are both good - our good being generated of his good. And therefore, his generation of life here on earth is to further the good of the universe.

H: What?

D: Yes. The reason for the creation of life is to further the existence of the good.

H: Whatever that is! And I suppose our existence is predicated on our furthering the good in the universe, and hence, our mandate is to do good? That's it?

D: Yes. That's it.

H: And not to be facetious, what good is doing or being "good?" I am having a problem seeing the significance of doing good.

D: First, the more capacity for information and knowledge that life possess, the more good it can do. Therefore this evolution toward a greater capacity to possess and assimilate information is of the good and was desired by the creator. A single-celled organism although good in itself is actually a stepping stone in evolution to developing species with a greater capacity to do good by its greater possession of information and knowledge.

H: You almost seem to infer that we are still evolving toward greater capacities of knowledge.

D: There is no doubt about it. We are outstripping our evolutionary speed of development and creating extended memory and information processing units to aid our cooperative production. And this is a type of evolution, non-genetic.

H: Yes, we are. There are anthropology professors here at the university that contend the same thing. But still, let's go back to this ultimate mandate of ours of doing good here on earth. Why do we need to do good? Why is it needed and are we by our own existence, that is, by just being here, of the good?

D: Yes, as long as we produce we are of good. Do you remember how we discussed previously when speaking of that which is ethical, that production is the purpose of ethical behavior?

H: Yes. That which produces is of the good and is ethical.

D: We are created to do good by sacrificing our time, energy, information/knowledge, amidst an environment of risk to produce that which further insures our survival and proliferation because our being comes from the good of the creator.

H: Let me ask you about the good that you keep speaking of. There are times when we, it seems, do not do good things. If we are of the good of the creator, how is it that we can do something not of the good. Let's say for example somebody commits a crime or somebody commits suicide. How is it that the non-good can exist when we are sprung from the good?

D: As we discussed in our disquisition of ethics, the existence of life in the universe entails necessarily the element of risk. All day long everyday we make decisions by assessing our situation as best we can along the standard of the good commensurate with the various risks attendant to each and every situation that we encounter as we live our daily lives.

H: Yes, I remember that in our discussion of ethics that since there is risk in this universe we cannot often make the best decision and that misery, failure, tragedy, downfall, or whatever lugubrious, negative thing we can think of may, can, or does happen in our lives. We work and sacrifice to make a living through producing what we can for a return of the means of a livelihood thereby rendering or usually insuring our survival - hopefully a survival without much misery - allowing us to procreate a family insuring the continuance of life.

D: Yes. And do you remember our standard for the good?

H: The good is that which is helpful to survival, first on the individual level which means that which helps the individual life entity survive, be healthy, and reproduce, and secondarily, on the social level whereby that which promotes a general good of collective individuals as society is needed to help insure the species in general and insure the continuation of life by its numbers. We all know that probability can cause the downfall of individuals easily enough as we have all lost someone close to us before that person's time. Numbers help insure the ultimate survival of life.

D: Yes.

H: But what of some anomalies with regard to this understanding of the good such as suicide? It isn't good, yet it happens, and it happens to the individual who is produced by the good of the life force. Or what about evil? I know we researched the meaning and essence of evil, but perhaps we could go over it again in light of my questions regarding the problems arising from the good of life.

D: Suicide, although bad on the social level, and certainly bad on the individual level as it destroys one's life, is done because the individual perceives it as the best thing in one's circumstances. It is because there is so much either physical or mental misery that the individual must do anything to escape it. Remember, we have a twofold purpose which is not only to survive individually and socially and ensure continuation, but also to fight misery, and this obligation invokes us to strive to get as far away from misery as possible. To answer the second half of your question, misery can arise from the good of creation because of the existence of risk inherent in the nature of life outside the divine. Circumstances can arise that place the individual in an unfavorable position whereby he must strive to extricate himself.

H: Why must we strive to reduce misery and position ourselves as far away as possible? You seem to indicate that this is some sort of moral obligation on our part.

D: This is due to our understanding of the good. It is best not only to survive at a subsistence level as did our ancestors of way long ago especially before the advent of farming but to take ourselves away from that and climb upward. Subsistence-level existence keeps us not far from death. If anything goes wrong, a person is finished; society does not proliferate.

H: Yes, I understand that under the aegis of science, we have come a long way: the medical field has certainly and dramatically increased the various survival rates, making our probability of staying alive after the occurrence of an injury or the incidence of disease: industry has made us comfortable with nice homes, cars, televisions, and the list is endless. But what I want to know is why, as you seemed to indicate, is there an incumbency to take ourselves in this direction; why must we improve our lot? And this question implies further inquiry: if there is an obligation that compels us to improve our condition, then there seems to be a requisite attitude on our part to seek pleasure, comfort, indulgence, and maybe even perhaps materialism.

D: It is incumbent on us to give ourselves the best living, and there is nothing morally wrong with owning things and striving for the good life. First, there is nothing wrong with it as it is of the good and keeps us far away from misery, death, and degradation. There is an incumbency to strive for pleasure and all that is of the good; because in the impartation of knowledge to the entropic molecules that enabled them to reverse course and became anti-entropic, the entropic molecules take on the ability to make decisions, and become life. And within the original decision to impart the knowledge of life, there is the will of the good. That is, this original decision to create life is of the good; the decision is born of the good and is willfully good, and we are the benefactors of this good. It is clearly a mandate of being created from a good willful act that we must strive for the good. Owning things and seeking pleasure are basically good things (but, of course, this must be taken in moderation just like everything else as too much of anything becomes destructive). Owning things and indulgence in pleasure are worthy objectives because the only ethically obtainable way to them is through production and the attendant effort and sacrifice that goes with it. In order to have pleasure you, or someone before you, must have worked to produce something in order to have the time and means to enjoy the benefits of production. The good has an attendant mandate to produce.

H: It seems that you are saying that as our creator was of the good in creating life that there is a mandate as his creation for us is to be of the good and the striving for pleasure and material things is of the good because it is born of the efforts and sacrifices of the production that enables us to enjoy these benefits. And so without production and the attendant efforts and sacrifices, there can be no earthly pleasure and no material things.

D: Yes.

H: This might be getting off the track or subject of our inquiry but theology points out that we are born in sin and you point out that we are born of the good.   Your philosophy seems to contradict theology.   And what's more, it seems that theology points out that materialism, hedonism, and the like are to be avoided, and your comments of pleasure and owning things seem to be close to a notion of materialism and maybe even hedonism.

D: First, being created of the good is separate from being born in sin.   The intent in creating life is tautologically good.   Creating life is good as the creator's original intent to produce life has to be of the good; it has to be an absolute in its goodness as it cannot be conceived otherwise.   If it were bad to create life it would set us all into ethical commotion, that is, we would not be able in our lives to strive for the ethically good.   This leaves us with the option that life's creation is neither good nor bad.   But this is inadequate also in that the impartation of knowledge to create life was a willful act with intent.   The intent must have a reference point or a standard attendant to it.   If not, then there is no basis today by which we can say that any behavioral act or deed is good or bad or can be judged in any way.   A standard has to be present at the beginning necessarily.   What is true at the beginning will be true throughout. You cannot in the interim development of life suddenly decide to change the standard by which life is known, judged, and operated by a mindful decree.

H: I see.

D: We know that ethically murder is wrong although killing sometimes can be justified.   But unadulterated murder without cause

- what I have heard to be called "murder one" - is wrong and we know it. We know it because life is good, precious, and important to us, and it must have been important to the creator as there was absolute goodness in the production of life on earth.

H: I think I see. Without the presence of good in life, there can be no judgment, no ethical standard as we know it. But what about the theological concept of sin and being born in sin?

D: As we noted, along with the presence of life is the existence of risk and free will to handle this risk. Although the production of life was and is good, life has to deal with its environment through its free will with the presence of risk, - and mistakes are made. Sin is a mistake that is made in apportioning the consequences of life's discretionary powers in making its decisions.

H: That is to say, sin is unethical behavior but that the intent of the existence of life is of the good.

D: Yes.

H: A few moments ago you said that in order for us to know ethical behavior there has to have been this good at the inception of life, and without it there would be no standard for judgment of behavior and that his original good is an absolute of sorts.

D: Yes, because the original act of somehow injecting into molecules the knowledge that started life and this intent of the knowledge to create life is good, the standard by which ethical behavior can be understood is born. And if we recall this standard in our past discussions, it is rooted in the survival of life. That which promotes the individual survival is good and that which promotes the societal survival and continuation of life is ethical - the ethical being of the good.

H: Yes, when we spoke of the ethical, we noted that the means by which societal survival is achieved is through cooperation that leads to production which brings us all our means to further and promote survival and brings us away from misery.

D: Yes. And so without that original intent that the creation of life was being of the good, we cannot conclude that ethics is founded in the good of behavior, this good being cooperation that promotes production so that we may take ourselves away from misery. Without this absolute standard, there is no good or bad in behavior. But we know that there is good and bad in behavior.

H: You spoke also a minute ago again about free will and the discretionary powers of decision-making. Let's go over the nature of free will again.

Chapter Five

Free Will

D: All right.

H: You mentioned previously that free will is the ability of the consciousness to choose according to its priorities which are based on its understanding of what is best for the individual in the struggle to exist and insure its continuation from the various options that are presented to the self.

D: Yes. That is basically it. As the life entities become more complicated so does the situation of existence. As the entities - or cellular entities with their small individual genetic consciousnesses - combine to make more complicated beings, the individual genetic consciousness for the sake of the greater organism's survival must give up some of its command to the discretion of the whole body of the cells in the form of a secondary consciousness whose purpose is to handle the various experiences from without in order for the cellular mass to continue to survive and for the primary genetic information to continue to be passed on.

H: Following that reasoning, the purpose of free will is to support the insurance of the passing of the information contained in the genes to the next generation. But surely, it seems to me that free will includes more than that or at least is more complicated than just the discretionary alignment of priorities in the struggle to strive and pass along the life force and its information contained in one's self. It seems to me that a normal insignificant action of daily life like going to see a friend or deciding which book to read or which car to choose to buy is far from the purpose for which you believe free will exists. These types of actions seem to be a matter of sheer taste and do not involve an alignment of priorities in the struggle to survive.

D: I agree in that at first glance it does not seem like it, but in essence it is. An action such as choosing a certain book to read, one's clothes to wear on a certain day, or what to buy or drive that day, or whatever other matter of taste is still included in our priority schedule. The deployment of taste by the self is still within the ken of the self in deciding how to live and survive throughout each day. As we have previously established we are a mixture of interior and exterior originating experiences and many of these interior originating ones dictate preferences that are offered by the exterior ones. But these preferences are manifestations of how the individual sees the world and his position within it.

H: But this does not explain the relation between the free will in choice of the color of our tie, sport coat, or car and our struggle to survive. We cannot reduce free will to the sole purpose of arranging our survival priorities. It seems to me that there is no connection between priorities for survival and what color our shirt should be in the morning.   Any of the shirts we choose are surely fine for survival.

D: Of course, any would be sufficient for survival as would whatever color that one would choose for a car.   They are all suitable for survival. But we are not to just survive, using the word in its strictest sense. We are to get as far away from misery as possible. For, the farther away we are, the more insurance we have from extinguishment, and thus, to survive. Hence, we are to survive well.

H: Yes, I remember going over that concept of separation from bare existence and abject misery and toward that which is the good, and the good being that which propels that which promotes survival. It is obvious that our striving for the betterment of man has enabled us, especially in this modern age to make great strides in providing a better quality of living for all. Everyone, except for maybe the ascetic who believes that in order to be mentally comfortable one cannot have physical comforts, wants to be comfortable in their life as comfort indicates an ease of living and surviving and proliferating one's genes.

D: Yes.

H: But this still does not explain the problem of taste.

D: When it comes down to which shirt you should wear when all the shirts are equally fit for wear, there are two additional parameters available to the free will. First is the aesthetic sense which will structure your tastes in life, and if you recall your own published notes from our discussions on aesthetics, you will note that the aesthetic is also based in survival. Our sense of beauty is an important step in our evolutionary development: its purpose is to enable us to see that which is the positive extreme; that which is beautiful is the most advanced or necessary thing that symbolizes the ultimate in our survival.

H: Yes. I recall our discussions. The aesthetic sense enables us to recognize the positive extreme. That which indicates to us the most desirous thing and/or actions for survival is the most beautiful. Hence, the Olympic diver is beautiful because he exemplifies the ultimate ability of the muscular coordination of the human body. The powerful body of the Arabian stallion exemplifies speed; the mathematical symbols produced by the great theoreticians such as Einstein, Planck, and Newton evince the ultimate in man's creative and mental capabilities. It is through our aesthetic sense that we appreciate such things, but still, I do not see how this relates to the color of my shirt in the morning or the design of the tie I choose, or the prettiness of the clothes that a girl would choose for a social occasion.

D: The aesthetic sense extends itself to normal everyday problems of taste. It enables us, of course, to see the beauty of the diver, but the same mental capacity enables us to order our personal tastes for us in our everyday lives.

H: How so?

D: Just as the aesthetic sense enables us to see that which is beautiful such as the appreciation of the gracefulness of the Olympic acrobatic figure skaters, the same intuitive ability allows us to make personal choices such as which clothes to buy and wear, which car to choose, or which fragrance a lady may prefer and so on. All these choices of taste are from the aesthetic sense. The individual chooses from his perception of what is the best-looking or most pleasing or beautiful. The girl picks out a dress and deems it pretty. It is her sense of aesthetics that enables her to sense the prettiness of her new dress. The aesthetic sense enables her to see the design of the dress which may have some pattern of flowers that she likes as she knows flowers are beautiful and she decides to incorporate this beauty into her exterior self in the form of a dress that she needs to wear to a social occasion as we are social animals and we need to be social in order to survive as we talked about in our discussion on ethics.

H: Yes.

D: So even in matters of which color to choose we are able to pick because our interior originating aesthetic experiences indicate that for today's purposes, when we will be outside in the hot sun, white would suit us, or this evening at the gala party, navy blue would be suitable and so on.

H: But are there occasions when no such operatives guide us to the decision, when all the circumstances appear to be the same, and yet we make a choice of this color or that, or we choose an egg sandwich to an egg omelet, or when a cheetah chooses from a herd of antelope one particular antelope to run down?

D: This is the second parameter that is present in choices of free will. It is probability. Sometimes when no operative influences come to us and it is six of one or a half dozen of something else, we choose just to choose and get past the decision. This final parameter is just the chance of minimal choice.

H: Then, free will of the consciousness is the license that the genetic information gives to the conglomerate cellular mass by which it may operate in unison furthering its survival. And the essence or operative standard by which this free will functions is the prioritization of the choices available to the living entity in each instant as time passes that furthers its chances of survival.

D: Yes.

H: I'm amazed because it seems from my own prejudiced personal view that I seem to be more than this.

D: Like what?

H: Well, let's take the problem of free will expressed in the polemics of theology. I understand that there are two sides to the debate. One side says that we possess free will in all our decisions and the other is of the opinion that when it comes to learning of the way to the Lord, there is no free will and that there are those who are chosen, or whoare, they become one of the elect; to wit, they become one of those given the impetus to be faithful and religious. In other words, do we come to believe in God because we have received divine direction to do so or do people believe out of their own free will? And I bring this problem up because it seems to involve predestination and determination for those who believe they are chosen to be of the elect. And if there are those who have been directed to believe in God, it seems that it is through divine communication to do so. If God directs someone to do something, then he can direct the future, and if he can direct the future, can God know the future?

D: He can know our every move and knows what we will do presently, but because of the existence of probability, risk, and uncertainty in the chaotic universe, He, as an observer, cannot know our particular futures since there is the system of free will which negotiates life as it occurs; and as life is in existence with a chaotic universe loaded with risk and probabilities, the future is never certain. If it were certain then everything is known and determined which would mean there is no existence of free will. But we know that free will does exist and its purpose is to negotiate the trial of the existence of risk and probability with the presence of life in the universe.

H: If all the laws and the mechanics of the universe are known, and given all the parameters of any situation where life is not present, it would seem that any situation could be predicted and known. For example, an earthquake could be accurately predicted as long as we know all the physical parameters along the entire fault and all the mechanics involved in producing an earthquake. At the micro-atomic level, we could know what is going to happen if we know completely all the forces and subatomic particles involved. What I am trying to establish here is that we can know and accurately predict the universe if all parameters, mechanics, and physical laws involved are known. If the universe is completely mechanical, governed by a specific set of laws, and if we know all the laws and parameters of any situation, we can predict with certainty what will happen, and the probability of the forthcoming event will approach one hundred percent.

D: Yes, that's correct. I suppose we could predict everything if we know everything, but quantum mechanics and the Uncertainty Principle will not allow an observer of the universe to know everything to start with.

H: Yes, I understand that. I was speaking hypothetically. Further, if life is involved, then there is certainly an element of probability. If in all situations we must make a decision as to what to do in our lives and there are elements in the decision that are equal, then life cannot make the decision clearly by just arranging its priorities. It will make the decision by just happenstance. When going one way or another is the same and we cannot perceive that there is an advantage to us in choosing one path or the other, then probability steps into our lives and we choose by just picking without rhyme nor reason and it would be impossible to predict what we would pick.

D: That's correct. But it would be possible to predict with a probability coefficient what life will do on the macro level if there is the absence of the equal alternatives and the chance decision. And on the micro level if one can know all the interior and exterior originating experiences of a particular life entity, one could know to a high degree of probability the outcome of the life entity's decision because all life's free will decision-making criteria is based on survival and the free will decision-making process arranges its priorities on what is best for its life and its passing of its genetic information to its successive generation.

H: Yes.

D: With regard to the theological problem of free will, it may be that some people receive divine inspiration. It is mentioned in the Bible and other writings that God has imparted communication with mortals and hence has directed them to do various things, whether he directs every single person who proceeds to have faith in his existence or not remains to be seen. It may be that he does, or it is just free will that takes us there or it may be a combination.

H: Yes, I suppose the important thing is that we understand the nature of free will. But I am still wary of whether we have examined it completely and that its nature has been entirely revealed.

D: There is not as much licensing in the mandate of the free will as one would think as the gene does not want to leave perfectly and completely its destiny in the hands of the free will of the group consciousness. The biological holders of life's information want to insure its survival and hence prompt the living entity with a plethora of interior-originating experiences that direct the entity to get its genetic information passed onward to a new generation insuring its continuation.   Hence, this life force, holder of the genetic information, only gives up to the consciousness enough authority in the form of free will which will promote its own particular interests which is to survive.

H: As I understand it, you purport that genetic factors have limited on purpose the amount of freedom of our free will to be free in making our decisions. In maintaining this point of view it seems that there is a consciousness at the genetic level that has a free will of its own and it has made the decision to pass along some discretionary decision-making capacities of its free will to another secondary consciousness.

D: Yes.   You will remember that wherever there is the assimilation of information for purposes of survival, there is consciousness.   And because at the cellular level, there is an assimilation of information or knowledge, there exists a consciousness, albeit minuscule.

H: And this tiny, but accumulative, consciousness when information has been amassed has allowed a certain area in living entities to form for the creation of a greater consciousness. It just seems to me that this consciousness is of the greatest importance and the result of some sort of design.   I, naturally, want to place significance on this because I want to feel important in this scheme of things, and I cannot help but feel that there is more to free will than what you have said.

D: Well, this may surprise you a bit, but you do not want it to be more; your free will is not more inclusive because within the conscious freedom to choose our priorities based on our needs in surviving is housed our entire ethic.   That is, everything that we discussed which you put down on paper in your tome, *The Nature of*

Ethics, is encapsulated in this area of the priority decision-making. And this standard based on our survival and the survival of our genetic information has evolved in us to the extent that we are perfectly suited to it and we are comfortable with it. Hence, you feel that it must be something more because you are happy with your consciousness and its existence. You feel perfectly comfortable with it, and the standard by which this consciousness operates in its daily decision-making process which employs what we call our free will in choosing at every situation what to do comes from our experiences which give us our understanding of that which is ethical.

H: And as we have already noted, ethics is the study of the good and bad in behavior.

D: Yes. And behavior is our manifestation of the actions resultant from our decisions based on our free will, which harbors our ethic, operating on its need to make decisions based on its needs in proceeding through the course of everyday life.

H: We don't seem so free after all. Our free will seems confined to our ethic and sense of aesthetics.

D: Precisely. We operate our reason and effort according to our understanding of our aesthetics and ethics and what we should do. We have received an ethic ultimately initiated when the first piece of knowledge was implanted into life's beginning entity or entities by our creator. There seems to be some argument precisely how this ethic evolved within us, but it is with us provided by the creator, and it suits us perfectly.

H: And it is within our free will that our ethic and this aesthetic sense is enslaved both of which are contained in the standard of the good which emanates from our ultimate mandate of survival.

D: Yes.   Upon presentation of choices available to us, our interior-originating experiences both biologically and culturally induced give us the standard by which free will may arrange the priorities to make the choice based on our survival in order to continue with our lives and go on to the next decision. Whenever a choice is needed the interior originating experiences of the ethic appear to provide the standard by which the consciousness of the free will may decide societal problems.

H: OK, you have stated that free will is the ability of the consciousness to choose according to its priorities which are based on the understanding of what is best for the individual in the struggle to exist and insure its continuation from the various options that are presented to the self. Now, according to what you have just said, somewhere in this definition there is housed a person's sense of aesthetics and his system of ethics, and all his priorities by which he is able to consummate his daily decisions that are tied to his will to survive. Perhaps, you could clarify how all this fits together.

D: Free will is reason plus effort of the consciousness to make decisions.

H: What? Free will is only that?

D: Yes.

H: This seems like a new definition.

D: Not really. I used the word "ability" before. But mental ability is the degree of effort and its power of reason. Physical ability is its degree of corporeal strength plus its execution of that strength.

H: OK.

D: These two tools, reason, and effort, of the consciousness combine to first establish the priorities according to the good as we talked about before. We know from our internal originating experiences that primary to our existence we must survive. Secondarily, to help us survive we need the cooperation of our fellow beings, and we must lend our cooperation to them in order to produce and insure our survival and the survival of mankind.

H: Yes, we discussed this in our conversation on ethics. So, we have a standard by which we know how to set our priorities in making a decision.

D: In all decisions, there is the primary parameter of the establishment of the priority and the secondary level of the chosen action, and free will establishes both. First, free will enables the consciousness to set up its priorities which are a series of preferences. For example, the consciousness has information that comes to it that indicates the feeling of hunger. It assimilates the information and recognizes that hunger appears after a while. The application of reason prioritizes the absence of hunger to hunger itself. Reason applied to the information of what hunger is leads us to the establishment of the priority of preventing its existence. This priority is obviously of the good.

H: Yes. Thus, we have established a priority.

D: Next, according to our information about hunger and allowing our reasoning to make an extrapolation we know that we will become hungry later on this evening, and hence, by the effort of applying reason we realize and decide to go down to the store to get something that will enable us to prevent this onslaught of hunger later.

H: Does every decision that we make involve a priority and then an action to get us through this process of living?

D: Yes, every decision requires the development of an action set against our priorities, and both the action and the priority were established by free will, or reason plus effort.

H: Reason plus effort applied to information produces priorities and a priority is a form of knowledge and with this knowledge, we are moved to actions that get us through life in the best way that we see fit for ourselves.

D: Correct.

H: And that's it? Free will is only reason and effort?

D: Yes.

H: I feel that we have become closer to an understanding, but I need to assure myself that I have a firm understanding.

D: Surely.

H: Let's go through some more examples of free will. In setting priorities how about the case when we do something we know we should not, such as when a person smokes cigarettes or drinks too many alcoholic beverages or even does something overtly dangerous such as driving too fast or skiing beyond one's ability? It seems in these cases reason and effort and free will were sometimes inoperative in setting up its priorities.

D: It is not that the system of free will and the decision-making process broke down. We are complicated, and conflicting desires and priorities can clash. Let's take your example of the smoker. The person knows that his cigarette gives him some short-term satisfaction and he is appreciative of it. He reasons that this pleasure is important and sets it into his scheme of priorities along with hunger for food and thirst for drink. It has a priority. The smoker does not want to be presented with the craving for a cigarette and hence can make decisions about smoking as to when he needs to buy the product and when to light up; however, you mentioned that he shouldn't be doing this.

H: Yes.

D: But he has not used his free will to divest himself of your priority for him. That is, it is your priority from your reasoning that over the long term smoking or heavy alcoholic beverage consumption or driving too fast is potentially inimical to that person's health. He, unfortunately, has not come to the same conclusion through his free will. He may not have considered the long-term consequences as you have through the use of your free will. He has established his short-term free will induced conclusion concerning his priority of smoking. Once he has established his priority, his daily decisions regarding smoking come easily.

H: You seem to equate free will with just thinking and making a decision.

D: Free will is just our reasoning facilities plus effort. It is just our effort in thinking about something.

H: But isn't that just what the creation of knowledge is? You said that knowledge is establishing the relationship between the separate experiences. It seems to me that assimilating informational experiences into new knowledge is but the free will in action as we know it so far.

D: Yes, the assimilation of knowledge is the free will acting on the incoming information.

H: So how does the assimilation and creation of knowledge, value, prioritization, and free will all fit together? It seems that free will is found in all of this.

D: Yes, it is.   Experience is the incoming stimuli to the consciousness and when these incoming stimuli are placed in memory, that is, an effort is made, a decision is effected - automatic or not - to place these experiences into memory, a priority already having been established to do so.

H: How could a decision have been made if these experiences were placed into memory automatically? It seems to me that if something is automatic, then it cannot be a conscious decision of one's free will.

D: If the action, in this case, the automatic placement of information into a memory, were effectuated, there could have been a decision made somewhere, notwithstanding it might have been automatic at its final level. Although it was ostensibly automatic, there was a decision earlier at a more basic level that prepared the consciousness to perform the placement into memory automatically. It may have been a genetic, cellular, or even divine decision that deemed it inappropriate for the consciousness to make the decision or have to make the decision. All the actions of an organism do not have to be decided at that level of consciousness. The consciousness would become too busy as biologists readily know. Evolution let many actions be decided at more primary levels of consciousness.

H: Hence, the evolution and development of the subconscious.

D: Yes.

H: So when information was placed into memory, a decision at some level was made, and of course, the decision was aided by the establishment of a priority which indicated that that information should be committed to memory. Hence, when the arrival of the information occurs, the decision is made to store it as it is understood that there is importance in the storage of this information.

D: Yes.

H: And this decision of the memory placement was made by free will - reason plus effort - at the conscious level, and possibly, it is automatic and effectuated at the subconscious level. When a decision is made, free will with its reason and effort is necessarily involved.

D: Correct. Knowledge is reason (mental faculties), effort (or will) plus experience (or information), and decisions are reason and effort, which is free will, together with information (or knowledge) and priorities (a kind of knowledge) plus an action.

H: I see. And priority?

D: A priority is reason and will - or free will - plus value.

H: And where does value come from? I suppose you mean Aristotle's "good?"

D: Yes. Value is that which we see as having importance to us in our daily living and surviving and of course is that which is good. It is knowledge of that which is good.

H: How do we come to know our values? Wherefore do these values and this goodness exist?

D: Well, if that which is valuable to us is that knowledge which we understand as good, then value equals free will plus information (knowledge) within which there is the standard of that which promotes our survival which is specific knowledge coming from interior originating experiences.

H: I don't understand.

D: Value is a sub-category of knowledge. If we have a value, then it is a piece of knowledge. This knowledge is that which promotes our well-being. All knowledge that is good for us and helps our well-being has value. So, a value is that knowledge which promotes our well-being.

H: OK. I think I see. Now, let me see if I have this correctly. Information is experience plus memory. Knowledge is reason plus effort plus information. Decisions are reason plus effort plus information plus priority plus action. A priority equals reason plus will plus value plus information and finally a value equals knowledge (a sub-category of).

D: Yes.

H: However, there seems to be a problem. "Decisions" is listed as free will plus information plus priorities and priorities are listed as free will plus value plus information. That means decisions would actually be free will plus information plus value plus free will and information again. This, of course, adds redundancies to the definitions and makes them, it seems to me, imprecise.

D: Good point. The answer lies in that we are dealing with sub-categories of knowledge. Priority is a kind of knowledge and decisions involve free will, knowledge (all kinds may be required) plus action to attempt to resolve the imminent situation. Hence, a priority is free will plus information that is germane to the priority plus the value which is a type of knowledge that the person has already established: it is free will applied to a specific type of knowledge. For example, much hunger is bad for our health, which causes us to set a priority in our own life of trying to avoid hunger. Therefore, we plan for meals to ensure our living pleasure.

H: It sounds like a priority is nothing but a value, and priority should be not reason plus will (free will) plus a value plus information, but just value. After all, just the knowledgeable conclusion that hunger in general should be avoided is a value and at the same time a priority in our lives.
D: There is not a big difference between priority and value as you are pointing out. It is only the personalizing of a value. Let us

take our hunger value. Reason, will, and information tell us that the prevention of hunger is valuable in the ability to survive and we decide to make it one of our personal values - or priorities - in our decision-making processes.

H: But wait. You just said that it is a decision to take a value and make it a personal value and your definition of priority stated that it was free will, value, and information. Now, you are introducing the factor of decision and the standard for decisions including priority which makes the definition circular.

D: Yes, we did not include decision into the making of priorities because we should separate decisions that require physical actions that are needed by us to survive and do well in the world, just as a mental decision has no meaning unless there is a resultant physical action that promotes our well-being. The mental decision-making process I will purport is in the reason and effort part of the priority standard. One's reason and mental effort will by itself make a value one's own. But our purpose here of analyzing these terms is to understand the nature of information, knowledge, and free will; and in doing so if it would make it a bit clearer to add into the definitions the distinction of mental and physical decisions, we can easily do so.

H: I see. We could easily say that decisions are free will, information, our values plus a manifest physical action. And a priority would be free will, information, and a value plus a mental action.

D: Yes. And these values are forms of knowledge that are resultant from our free will and information. Priorities have a different time frame. They were already established previously. It is the same free will but a different time and the same is true for information. You could denote the various components by using the sub-nomenclature of say information (T1) or free will (T2) where T denotes time.

H: Let me bring up again the issue in Christian theology circles of whether one is chosen to be a believer and have faith or whether it comes through our free will. With what we know of free will is there anything that we can add to this polemic? I know for my part that there was an internal originating experience one day that caused me to think that one should not be considered in the Western hemisphere a well-read person if one has not read at least part of the Bible's Old Testament and the gospel of the New Testament. Therefore, I proceeded to peruse parts of the OT and all of the NT and I was so impressed by it that I began to go to church on Sunday. But still, even though I now know what free will is, I cannot come to any conclusion as to this free will versus the elect in the problem of faith and religion.

D: Both are present and available to all persons, but the degrees to which they are present vary. The elements to this problem are not mutually exclusive.

H: I do not follow you.

D: All people at least to some degree have some interior originating experiences that indicate to the self a cognizance of some knowledge of religion, faith, and God, and the existence in this world of theological polemics. For example, you were aware that the Bible is an important literary work, to say the least, and being intellectually active you thought that you could not be intellectually well-rounded unless you made an effort to read at least the Gospel of the New Testament. The seed of the thought of the Bible followed by the application of free will and the decision and its subsequent action of reading the Bible produced a churchgoing man.

H: Yes. There seems to be the seed of interest and the free will to search further.

D: You had an interior originating experience to which reason was applied making a piece of knowledge. This experience and then knowledge could very well have been immediately attributable to the creator, the Lord, or it may have been an intermediate thought originating from others before it, but ultimately attributable to the creator somewhere as certainly the first knowledge was from him, and other knowledge after that has been known to directly emanate from the creator, our Lord.

H: You are speaking of religious experiences that people have at various times related to or of some sort of divine intervention.

D: Yes. It has varied from something as seemingly insignificant as the experience of the Apostles receiving the teachings or Paul's divine communication from Jesus on the road to Damascus or Mohammed's experiences. But it seems that almost all people have an innate interest in religious matters and wonder about the origins and the hereafter of life and the universe, and it is free will that works or does not work, on this interest, and finally, we come to some conclusions as to the personal development of a faith.

H: You seem to indicate that at least to some degree we are all available to be elected, but in order to consummate it, our free will needs to develop our faith.

D: Yes. And I believe this conforms to Scripture in that we know that the elect are referred to, but at the same time the Bible is rife with inferences of the existence of free will not the least of which would be Jesus 'bidding to Paul for the need to exhort to the Jews and gentiles alike the good news.

H: So as I understand it, the potential to be elected is within almost everybody, if not all, and the free will of the individual is what enables anyone to develop his faith.

D: Yes. Free will plays the major part except in the cases where the seed of the interest in faith or the divine experience is so powerful that it diminishes the importance of the free will.

H: And those cases would be those who have been blessed with strong primary religious experiences such as Paul, the Apostles, and others.

D: Yes.

H: Then let me divert the conversation to another subject regarding free will. If there is true free will, then no one can know but maybe he can predict, what anybody will do. But if free will is just reason and effort, then perhaps it can be known what life will do in the future and the future is actually determined. In order for me to clearly understand free will I must be able to see that things are not determined, that no one can know what we do. Probably an observer can predict with a certain noted probability what a person might do, but this observer cannot know with a one hundred percent assuredness of our next move. Should an observer be able to know with one hundred percent certainty, then I may conclude that we do not have pure free will and that what we do is pre-determined and could be known. It further seems that if we have pure free will, then it can only be predicted what we will do in life, and this probability of knowing what our decision will be will range from very low to just shy of one hundred percent, but can never be perfectly known in advance.

D: Yes. You are right.

H: However, I am not convinced that we have pure free will; it may be that things are rolling along, unabated in a predetermined manner. Who is to say that an omniscient observer could not know what I will do next year, or what classes I will elect, or what my next move will be in a chess game? Is it possible to be an omniscient observer and one who knows the future?

D: The creator, our Lord, certainly is an omniscient observer of the present but not of the future. In the quantum mechanical world, as already noted, we know from the Uncertainty Principle that an observer cannot know everything about the action of particles. As the scale of the universe being observed widens, we know that the uncertainty diminishes and the probability of our general predictions tends to advance as our knowledge and our awareness increase. And when it comes to life, an observer, because of free will, cannot know for certain what decisions of action a life entity will make until, or just before, the point of the decision.

H: Why? What is the essence of the free will that makes certainty for the observer impossible?

D: Free will is reason plus effort, and our decisions are free will, information, and priorities (values). An observer cannot know what a life entity will do because he cannot have all the information and know all the interior originating experiences that the life entity has which includes the faculty of reason.

H: Why not?

D: In order to do so, he would have to be observing all the experiences that are happening at our consciousness. He would have to be experiencing everything we are experiencing simultaneously. If an observer were to do this, then he would be able to know what we would do just or at the moment we were to do it. And if an observer were to be able to experience everything we are experiencing, then he would actually be present, simultaneously aware of our consciousness just as we are. His consciousness would be the same as ours and would have to have the same consciousness. And since we rarely know what we will do very far into the future, an observer, even an omniscient one, would not be able to know also, not having all the information.

H: Then we would not be able to know the future of life as we cannot ever get enough information, and if life were to start again. it could not be predicted as to its unfolding and how it develops. He would only be able to predict using probability.

D: These questions require an answer in two parts at two different levels. First, it is just as in quantum mechanics and the Uncertainty Principle: we cannot know everything about a particle's behavior but as the scope of observation enlarges, our confidence of prediction and comprehension of the behavior of the universe increases. We can know that the earth will go around the sun, entropy will occur, gravity will draw smaller things to larger things. Although the existence of free will with the admixture of risk, probability, and the unavailability of information of the experiences at the individual consciousness level will prevent an observer from knowing what will happen in the next instance, we can predict with greater accuracy actions as they widen in scope. Hence, if life were wound up again and started, we would be able to know how baboons will act in general when meeting leopards or how ants will search for food at close to one hundred percent assurance. We will know that people will reproduce, raise children, work, and strive to produce goods and services to better their lives. However, whether a particular individual will follow this track of behavior, we may not be entirely sure. Therefore, we cannot know if a particular argument, altercation, fight, or war will occur, but we know over time they will occur in life. All these things are determined or will occur in general but not in the specific. If life were to reoccur with the present biological trappings in place, all the general behavior (but not divine) will reoccur including such great calamities as wars but the specifics would vary. In a reoccurring world, Hitler would not appear a second time, but strife of all degrees would from good to evil. Hence, it is determined that the general happenings of life occur, but the specifics are not of determinism because of the existence of free will, risk, and the unavailability of all relevant knowledge to the individual consciousness. As there is a compartmentalization of information and experience, the particulars of the individual consciousnesses remain unknown, unpredictable, and undetermined.

H: You say that actually the macroscopic course of life's behavior is determined?

D: Yes. It is by the informational parameters that have been set forth in our biological makeup. These parameters dictated by knowledge instilled into the genetic code prescribe macro-behavior. This combined with life socializing and the existence of free will with the vagaries of existence of all that is within the universe (risk) gives the assurance that macro-things will occur necessarily but specific things will be unknown as to whether they will occur at all.

H: Well, if there is any determinism in the universe then I suppose its source must be the creator's. But, if you say that there is some determinism, and it is of the creator's, then life must have been part of this determinism. Furthermore, if you say that the general makeup, behavior, actions, or patterns of life are determined, then these patterns are also the doing of a creator. And I understand, as we have already pointed out, that the initiation of life had to involve the dispensation of knowledge to the situation in order to overturn the presence of the entropic behavior of atoms and molecules. But this does not foretell in a deterministic way the presentation of life as we have it today. That is, the fact that we have evolved from simple life into complicated beings with our present behavior and existence does not seem to me to be determined.

D: If the creator's last step was just to turn the tide of the first molecules from entropic to life force possessive anti-entropic molecules, then I might agree with you. But probability states that this is not the case.

H: Are you referring to the recent spate of literature indicating that the naturalistic evolution that we have all been taught in school when studying Darwin does not explain completely and comprehensively the course of evolution?

D: Yes.

H: I am aware of this literature and its indications that just the naturally occurring mutations of genes are not capable enough, if at all, to supply the additional genetic information needed to enable life to construct the complicated, irreducible systems that are present, such as the eye or blood clotting or a myriad of other systems within us and the systems within much of life right down to the single cell.

D: That's correct.

H: I was much impressed by the literature's explanation of how complicated life's basic unit is, the cell. The structures within are so complicated and irreducible that the ability, inherent in the genetic code when reproducing itself, of producing new combinations would not be able to come up with the new irreducible systems needed by life to evolve. Hence, I take it that this indicates that not only was the creator present at the very first stage when he imparted knowledge to one or more molecules to allow them to go from the entropic to anti-entropic but was present further down the line throughout the development of life. It seems these developments lie way outside the ability of just raw probability to offer and require absolute raw knowledge in order to occur.

D: Precisely.

H: I agree because if we accept that the first step of the existence of knowledge was needed to trip the occurrence of the initial molecules going from the entropic to the anti-entropic, then the additional occurrence of knowledge to further enhance the beginnings of life is easily accepted. Life must carry knowledge, or consciousness would be nothing. But this leads me to another question. It seems to me that knowledge could be self-generating. Could it not be that once the thing is set in motion that life could not have somehow self-generated this knowledge all along the way throughout its own evolution, it just needs that first step of requiring the ability to go anti-entropic?

D: Any change outside the realm of probability's capacity to generate requires information and free will. Change requires this.

H: Does that mean that all life-oriented change outside that which can be affected by probability requires knowledge because, after all, free will plus information equals knowledge as we have already established?

D: Yes. If you are outside the influence of probabilistic events, then change can only be affected by knowledge.

H: But everything is subject to probability. It is possible that these events such as naturalistic evolution could have occurred even though there is now some evidence that the production of complicated irreducible systems, where if one part of many are missing the whole system does not function, such as blood clotting or the immune system, and would require a tremendously large and complex change in the DNA information server of the cell to effect. Probabilities, that the cell's DNA strand could just mutate to the extent in a short period of time naturally without any additional knowledge that it could produce the new system almost all at once because just producing part of it at one time does not allow the system to function and gives it no selective advantage are remote, to say the least. And as the complexity of the system grows so does the remoteness of the probability that it is affected by mere mutation or chance.

D: And as the greater the need for mutation to occur to provide the raw change that is needed in order to build these irreducible systems grows, correspondingly, there is a greater propensity for the gene population to produce deleterious characteristics that quickly get selected out of the population due to their non-adaptational characteristics.   As the need for the probability for positive mutations arises, so does the probability of the occurrence of deleterious outcomes grow, and hence, a non-adaptational, non-survival ratio in the gene pool increases and the number of individuals of the population that do not survive grows and places an increase of a general survival burden on this population leading it toward extinction.

H: It seems we are talking about one probability versus another: it is just that one is a high probability and one is a low probability.

D: But something happened, and if it happened, it is not subject to probability. It is just our perception of the problem or event that is subject to probability; it may just be that some probabilities are so high that we do not bother to pursue them anymore such as whether the earth goes around the sun.

H: Okay, we have strayed. Let's get back to the problem of whether knowledge can be generated within the organism producing the effected changes internally that would allow it to generate the systems of life that have evolved and further whether knowledge is self-generating in general.

D: Knowledge is limited by free will and the other parameters. The more the capacity for reason, effort, stimuli, and memory, the more the capacity for the production of knowledge. All are limiting factors.

H: OK.

D: But all change is effected by decisions performed within the consciousness by the free will operating on its stored knowledge and information. And so, in order that an organism to have the ability to change its genetic information server it requires a consciousness capable of taking in information from the environment demanding a change that would accommodate the organism to the environment or allowing it a new opportunity for expansion into another ecological niche. That is, informational stimuli would be provided by the environment which would be taken in by the consciousness which also would be tabulating stimuli and information at the genetic level where the effect will be made as the effect will require know-how by the consciousness to effect. It may be possible that such a system is in place in living organisms and biology has yet to discover its existence.

H: It seems that knowledge or information must be taken from the environment and taken to the genetic information server for indoctrination there. It certainly does not seem that there is an apparent free will around that has done this for the evolution of life, and it seems unlikely that sheer probability could have done this to such a degree of completion. The thought that probability produced such complicated organisms seems more and more unlikely. However, it seems more likely that the original consciousness that effected the first transmogrification of molecules going to the anti-entropic affected a system by which life's complicated systems could evolve. After all, if this consciousness is capable of the first step, then being able to assimilate the imputes from the environment to affect the genetic informational server is more likely and highly possible for this consciousness.

D: Yes. I agree. Change in life must be directed for the most part. Life by its free will must make decisions for its own survival and if these decisions are diluted by probability then life heads for its own entropy and death.

H: I don't understand.

D: The more life's decisions are directed by probability and not by consciousness, the more it becomes like entropy, or that is, the more it becomes entropic which is inimical to life. Life and its agent, free will, must do the decision-making.   The more a population places its reliance on just probabilistic mutational events to secure its evolution to an adaptative situation, the more it heads toward entropy and extinction. This is because change to the good requires the free will of a consciousness. Just random change is the same as entropy and hence the positive, good changes that can arise out of just random events are small compared to the number of deleterious results of random events which are entropic in nature. Consequently, if a system, biological or otherwise, is relying on a random entropic method to produce benefits for itself the amount of the entropy-influenced deleterious events will certainly far outweigh any random positive ones and put a tremendous anti-survival burden on the population.

Chapter Six

Existence From The Good

H: Let's proceed to return to our list of things we know to get back to my question of our purpose of being or why life exists.

D: We have already discussed that we are created to do good and that the good is of the ethic that has been provided to us from its implantation into our interior originating experiences confirmed by cultural or verbal exhortations by-products such as the Bible and other great writings throughout history.

H: Yes.

D: We have evolved an ethic to live to produce by cooperation using the vehicle of respect as we discussed in detail and as you have delineated in your writings. And our experience, we now know, is intentional as we are the purposeful and intentional product of a father who instilled knowledge into molecules causing them to go anti-entropic. This instillation of knowledge came from the intent of the good for the purpose of some good. Therefore, we know that the purpose here is to do good in our lives. This good is based on our survival and the survival of us as a group; its mechanisms being the passing of our genetic information to succeeding generations ensuring the continuation of life. This continuation of life is confirmed and insured by our doing good, and hence, all living things have an ethic of the good. It is just that ours is the most complicated as it rests upon extensive cooperation based on respect of others in our society based on the importance of their production.

H: Yes, I am following this.

D: And therefore, the Father's purpose of our existence must also be of the good. That is, the good of our existence is predicated on the good of the Father as his existence is predicated on the good. His being is good and his work and production are for the good: we are the recipients of his good in that we have received existence which we enjoy; but further, because we exist for the good and our good and existence is from the Father, our creator, and we are for his good also, there is a purpose for which we exist and that purpose is for the good not only of ourselves but of our Father's, our creator's also. This is confirmed in the Bible as it states that there is a purpose for mankind, and we know that the purpose is good - whatever it is - and it emanates from the Father, and therefore if the purpose is good and intentional, then it has merit or provides goodness for the Father also - to whatever degree we cannot know.

H: We are good for our creator? Our existence is beneficial for the Father?

D: As our good and the good of all life is based on our survival and this good came of the Father, his good is of the same essence. In some way, whether it is of little or immense proportions, we play some part in the good of the creator. And because our existence and the existence of life in general here on earth has some good attached to it for the creator, we may have solace in this fact. Life appreciates its existence, as we all know, and we humans appreciate it to the extent that we offer our thanks to the creator for it. We exist according to his purpose, we appreciate it, we give whatever thanks that we can or are capable of, and strive to be appreciative of being a part of his creation and goodness to whatever degree that is.

H: So, we actually somehow benefit the creator?   Isn't that somewhat a bold statement to say that we help or benefit or even that it was an ethical act to create us?

D: It has to be a good act. Life could not have been created of the bad.   And if we were created from his purposes, then those purposes are of his good.

H: What do you mean by "his good?"

D: Good is, as we have discussed, that which promotes survival and extends the distance between misery and living well. Therefore, we and life in general somehow extend or promote this well-being of our creator's.

H: I see.

D: And most likely he is here at least somewhat to be part of life's promotion to his purposes however small the increment of the good that we provide. He is here amongst the life on earth, amongst the good. And this good is true to the extent of its relevancy of this world and universe as we know it.

H: Do you think there is the continuation of our consciousness after our physical death?

D: We have two indications that lend credence to this belief or faith: first is that our interior originating experiences produce a desire for it and thoughts about it, and the second indication is that there have been messengers, prophets, and a messiah in history that proclaim this. They claim, as their source, communication - direct or indirect - from the creator. These are not proofs but indications. But we know that our existence is based in the good of the creator and indications, as strong as these, are not fleeting, but real, hard experiences. As the existence of life is of the good from his good, and as these indications are not whimsical but persistent interior and exterior originating experiences, then we can expect that our faith, at least somewhat to some life, will occur and manifest itself in the resurrection of some life with some of its attendant experiences after its physical death.

H: What do you mean "life with some of its attendant experiences?"

D: I am referring to our brief discussion noting that we have little without the memory of our experiences. If suddenly we lose our memory of our past experiences, then it is as if we did not exist before and we existed from the time we began to remember. Of course, we may have existed before that point, but it is no longer part of our consciousness and no longer relevant to our present consciousness. Further, if we were to have the memory window close upon us where experiences are retained, we could be given a new body or even a new existence whereby memory is available, and we would be none the wiser.

H: You mean that should a person be deprived of memory and die, the person's I (I use this pronoun for lack of a better expression - or perhaps "one's being" would be better) could be transplanted to a different physical plant with memory and the I, or one's being, would be again functional without awareness of a previous life, if you will.

D: Yes. And let me add I am not proposing that this actually happens, the point here is that without the memory of prior experience, our consciousness becomes separate from its previous consciousness.

H: But to return to our purpose here on earth I take it that we are to do good. And I take it that our Father's purpose in his creation of us is in some way to his good, but we cannot know to what good it is nor to what extent.

D: Yes.

H: And it can be concluded that there is or can be a resurrection, but to whom in specific or in general we cannot know.

D: We have hope. To this, each individual will be left to a faith in this eventuality. And for this, one must prepare the best he can and seek out his faith to his best satisfaction should he be interested in his resurrection and perpetual survival.

H: Yes. Pascal seemed to indicate that if we are interested in our resurrection, our best choice is to go to church and have faith.

D: I agree.

H: Thank you, Detmar. I have, as always, enjoyed this interview immensely. I am, as a result of it, hopeful and cheery. I look forward to the next time we shall meet.

D: I will also look forward to it. Good day, Haskell.

H: Good day.

www.ingramcontent.com/pod-product-compliance
Lightning Source LLC
Chambersburg PA
CBHW051323120626
46547CB00015B/2369